THE
TABASCO
COOKBOOK

The Tabasco Cookbook

RECIPES WITH
AMERICA'S FAVORITE PEPPER SAUCE

Paul McIlhenny with Barbara Hunter

FOREWORD BY JOHN BESH

PHOTOGRAPHS BY IAIN BAGWELL

Clarkson Potter/Publishers
New York

www.crownpublishing.com
www.clarksonpotter.com

CLARKSON POTTER is a trademark and POTTER with
colophon is a registered trademark of Penguin Random
House LLC.

Originally published in hardcover in different form in the
United States by Clarkson Potter, an imprint of the Crown
Publishing Group, a division of Penguin Random House LLC,
in 1993.

TABASCO® is a registered trademark for sauces and other
goods and services; TABASCO, the TABASCO bottle
design and label designs are the exclusive property of
McIlhenny Company, Avery Island, Louisiana, USA 70513.
www.TABASCO.com

Library of Congress Cataloging-in-Publication
is available upon request.

ISBN 978-0-7704-3539-4
Ebook ISBN 978-0-7704-43540-0

Printed in China

Book design by Ken Crossland
Cover design by Michael Nagin
Cover photographs by Iain Bagwell

All photographs copyright © 2016 by Iain Bagwell except
as noted. Photographs on pages 5, 6, 9, 16, 30, 87, and 142
copyright © 2016 by Eric Kiel.

10 9 8 7 6 5 4 3 2 1
Second Edition

We dedicate this book to members of the McIlhenny family who have preserved and nurtured our famous pepper sauce, and to generations of employees, distributors, and others who have taken such pride in producing Tabasco Sauce and making it available throughout this world—and even in outer space.

Contents

FOREWORD · 8
BY JOHN BESH

PREFACE · 10

ORIGINAL INTRODUCTION · 12
BY PAUL MCILHENNY

BREAKFAST & BRUNCH · 17

SOUPS, STARTERS & DRINKS · 31

MAINS · 57

SIDES & SAUCES · 103

DESSERTS · 133

COME VISIT US! · 141

MAIL-ORDER SUPPLIERS · 141

INDEX · 143

Foreword

Growing up, as I did, on the bayou in Louisiana one never expended much energy pondering such things as a favorite pepper sauce or football team. No, certain things such as these were just a given. As much as we knew who we'd cheer for on Sundays in the fall, we were born with a sense of what hot sauce belonged in the red beans, po' boys, gumbo, jambalaya, eggs, grits, Bloody Marys, or, for that matter, on our tables and in our pantries. As much as we love our state we were equally proud of our brand of pepper sauce—Tabasco—which had been our culture's ambassador to every corner of the globe. We were proud of our Avery Island, where Tabasco has hailed from since 1868, as well as of the McIlhenny family, who brought us the little red bottle full of great big flavor.

Long before I had ever met a McIlhenny, we spent many family picnics on the beautifully manicured grounds and in the lush tropical gardens of the Island, which is just a stone's throw from New Iberia, Louisiana. As soon as I would cross the little bridge onto Avery Island, tears would form as I'd take a big whiff of the salty air perfumed by the fermented peppers that gave an obvious nod to the main function of the land. For decades now I've known the family that calls Avery Island home, in particular its former patriarch, Mr. Paul McIlhenny, who was a larger-than-life husband, father, businessman, friend, hunter, and conservationist who also happened to produce the finest pepper sauce in the world. He was passionate about all things Tabasco and believed in the brand so much that he decided to expand it with additional sauces, foods, and products to share with the world, creating a Tabasco lifestyle— one that's built on good times with family and friends and, of course, big bold Louisiana flavors.

Aside from being the iconic businessman that he was, Paul worked tirelessly to shape his world into a better one by using his brand and resources to make positive changes in the environment, especially in our coastal wetlands. He encouraged me and others to not only join in his efforts, but also to decide what legacy we'd leave for future generations to enjoy—and to pursue those efforts with vigor and enthusiasm.

Along with the Tabasco line of products that brought Louisiana to the world, Paul used his gift of Cajun comedy, deep laughter, and *joie de vivre* to connect with people everywhere. I've come now to learn from my late great friend that a keen sense of stewardship and a great sense of humor can in fact make the world a better and tastier place. Today, as I cross the bridge onto Avery Island, my eyes still tear, though not because of fermented peppers, but for the remarkable legacy that Paul McIlhenny left us. A smile forms on the edge of my lips every time I unscrew the cap of my favorite pepper sauce, knowing that he lives with us at our table, making great food taste just a little bit better.

—John Besh

Preface

In February 2013, the business and culinary world lost Paul McIlhenny, former president and then chairman and CEO of McIlhenny Company. A gourmet and bon vivant, Paul, who was my second cousin once removed, excelled in his free time as a wild game and fish cook. He counted among his friends such food-world luminaries as Emeril Lagasse, Jacques Pépin, Ella Brennan, Paul Prudhomme, and R. W. Apple, Jr. In 2010, the James Beard Foundation inducted him into its Who's Who of Food & Beverage in America.

Back in 1993, however, Paul teamed up with McIlhenny Company's longtime public relations manager Barbara Hunter to compile the first edition of *The Tabasco Cookbook: 125 Years of America's Favorite Pepper Sauce*. Although twenty years have passed since then, *The Tabasco Cookbook* remains popular with and relevant to do-it-yourself home chefs. Yet not too long ago Paul observed the need for a second, revised-and-expanded edition of the cookbook, and he authorized work to begin revamping it.

On the eve of Tabasco's sesquicentennial, I'm therefore pleased to present here the result of that effort: the second edition of *The Tabasco Cookbook*. And while new recipes replace some of those found in the original edition, this book remains very much the book that Paul intended—a collection of select recipes that he enjoyed during a lifetime of good eating.

As before, many of the recipes reflect the South Louisiana culture that Paul so cherished. He grew up, after all, in the American culinary mecca of New Orleans and lived most of his adult life on Avery Island, his ancestral home in the rural Cajun and Creole section of the state. Other recipes reflect how most Americans love to cook today, with plenty of game-day and grilling favorites, pasta, and even desserts. Best of all, we've added new color photography of the delicious food as well as beautiful shots taken around Avery Island.

We think you'll agree that this volume will spice up your kitchen as heartily as a bottle of our renowned pepper sauce.

As Paul himself was fond of writing, "Hot regards from Avery Island!"

Sincerely,

Tony Simmons
President & CEO
McIlhenny Company

Original Introduction
by Paul McIlhenny

Time was when you could tell the length of a marriage by the level of Tabasco Pepper Sauce left in the bottle. Not anymore. The distinctive piquant flavor of everyone's favorite pepper sauce has firmly established it as a staple ingredient in contemporary cooking. But most people don't realize that there are almost 150 years of history in every little red bottle, going all the way back to the Civil War.

It all began on Avery Island, one of five islands rising in mystical fashion above the flat Louisiana Gulf Coast. The Island literally sits atop a mountain of solid salt, once supplying quantities of this valuable commodity to the Confederate states and prompting a Union attack on the geological oddity in 1862.

After the war, my great-grandfather Edmund McIlhenny, known to us as Grandpère, returned to the Island. According to one family tradition, he had been carefully nurturing a special verity of red capsicum peppers from Mexico or Central America. Grandpère delighted in the spicy flavor of these special peppers, which had, surprisingly, survived the wartime neglect of the Island.

He experimented with making a pepper sauce by crushing the ripest, reddest peppers, adding half a coffee cup of Avery Island salt per gallon, and letting the concoction age in crockery jars. When thirty days had passed, he added "the best quality French white wine vinegar" and, occasionally stirring each batch carefully by hand, let the mixture age for another thirty days so the flavors could intermingle. After straining the sauce, he corked the bottles, sealed the tops in green sealing wax, and sent the finished product to market with metal sprinkler fittings, to be inserted through the corks by consumers.

"That Famous Sauce Mr. McIlhenny Makes" lent welcome excitement to the monotonous diet of the Reconstruction South, and before long it was in such demand that he decided to market it commercially. In 1868, Grandpère grew his first commercial pepper crop and early the next

An 1857 portrait of Edmund McIlhenny, better known as Grandpère, who first created Tabasco Sauce in 1868.

year began sending bottles of his pepper sauce under the trademark Tabasco to grocers and wholesalers on the Gulf Coast and beyond. To his delight, the orders poured in.

Today, when the demand for spicy, well-seasoned food is even greater, people appreciate the fact that the aged capsicum peppers used for Tabasco Sauce give it a richer flavor, as well as a notable heat level. In fact, Tabasco Sauce scores 2,500 to 5,000 units on the Scoville scale, the standardized yardstick of hotness in food. And while other sauces often compensate for their lack of flavor and heat with more salt, Tabasco Sauce has about a fifth to a quarter of that of other pepper sauces, making it a great way to enhance flavors while reducing sodium.

Tabasco Sauce is still made today much as it was in Grandpère's time. Ripe peppers are crushed immediately after harvest, mixed with Avery Island salt, and aged in white oak barrels for up to three years. The peppers are then drained, blended with high-quality all-natural vinegar, and stirred for

Tabasco factory worker preparing a barrel of pepper mash, ca. 1955.

several weeks. Finally the sauce is strained, bottled, and sent out across America and the world.

South Louisiana is renowned for many things—swamps and bayous, alligators and muskrats, jazz and Bourbon Street, politics and preachers, Mardi Gras and Cajun fais-do-do dances, and most of all good food. We take great pleasure in both the preparation and enjoyment of our unique cuisine, an integral part of our culture. Many of our local specialties are neither low in fat nor quick and easy to prepare, but they are awfully good.

Here we've included what we believe to be the best of these recipes. Additionally, we give you favorite dishes collected over the years from many sources. In most recipes Tabasco Pepper Sauce is used as a flavor enhancer. If you want your food spicier, add more pepper sauce while making the dish or sprinkle it on at the table. We hope you will enjoy this collection and urge you to send us your favorite recipes—especially those that might call for a well-known brand of pepper sauce made on Avery Island.

PIQUANCY SCALE

By piquancy we mean an agreeable pungency or stimulation of the palate, not just heat or bite. The tiny Tabasco Sauce bottles numbering from one to four, which appear at the top of each recipe, are intended only as guides to the level of piquancy in the dish. Tabasco Sauce actually rounds out and enhances other flavors, contributing complexity and high notes where other pepper sauces only add heat. Even a recipe with a "four-bottle" rating won't blow you away, so if you like food very spicy, add more Tabasco Sauce to your own taste. Remember, the perceived degree of heat in food is very subjective; what is hot to one person may be mild to another.

 **= gives flavor a lift**

= a touch of heat

 **= definite authority**

= not for the meek

BREAKFAST
& BRUNCH

Rudy's Cheese Omelets à la Suds

For decades, Rudy Stanish, celebrated as "the Omelet King," turned out hundreds of omelets at a time for New York high society and charity functions. He always added Tabasco Pepper Sauce to his egg mixture. This cheese omelet recipe was one of his favorites.

      6 large eggs
      ⅓ cup beer
      ½ teaspoon Tabasco Pepper Sauce
      3 tablespoons butter
      3 tablespoons grated Parmesan cheese

In a large bowl, whisk together the eggs, beer, and Tabasco Sauce only until blended, not frothy.

   In a 9-inch omelet pan, melt 1 tablespoon of the butter over medium heat. The pan is hot enough when a drop of water spatters in it. Pour one-third of the egg mixture into the pan. Holding the pan handle in one hand, move the pan in a back-and-forth motion; with the other hand, use a fork to stir the egg mixture in a circular motion, about seven times. Sprinkle the omelet with 1 tablespoon of the Parmesan. To turn out the omelet, place your hand under the pan handle with your palm upward. Tip the pan and roll the omelet out onto a plate.

   Repeat twice more with the remaining egg mixture, butter, and cheese. Serve with additional Tabasco Sauce, if desired.

SERVES 3

Fresh Corn Pudding

This simple but delicious fresh corn custard gets a boost from a lacing of Tabasco Sauce and a sprinkling of paprika.

> 2 cups whole milk
> 1 tablespoon butter, plus more for the baking dish
> 3 large eggs
> ¼ cup all-purpose flour
> ¾ teaspoon salt
> 1 teaspoon Tabasco Pepper Sauce
> 2 cups fresh corn kernels, cut from the cob
> ¾ cup coarsely chopped red or green bell pepper
> Paprika

Preheat the oven to 325°F. Butter a deep 2-quart baking dish.

In a small saucepan, scald the milk, then stir in the butter and remove from the heat.

In a small bowl, whisk the eggs until foamy, then beat in the flour, salt, and Tabasco Sauce. Gradually beat in the warm milk mixture. Add the corn and bell pepper and mix well. Pour the mixture into the baking dish and sprinkle the top generously with paprika.

Set the baking dish in a larger pan, then add hot water to the larger pan until it comes 3 inches up the sides of the baking dish. Bake for 1 hour 15 minutes, or until the point of a knife inserted in the center of the pudding comes out clean. Let the pudding stand for 10 minutes before serving.

SERVES 4

Spicy Spinach Quichettes

To save time, make the spinach and scallion mixture the evening before and refrigerate overnight.

> 1 tablespoon olive oil, plus more for greasing the pan
> 2 cups chopped spinach
> 2 green onions, chopped
> 2 large eggs
> 1 cup heavy cream
> 1½ teaspoons Tabasco Pepper Sauce
> 1 teaspoon salt
> ½ cup shredded Cheddar-Jack cheese blend
> 1 16-ounce package refrigerated piecrust

Preheat the oven to 400°F. Grease 24 cups of a mini muffin pan.

In a 12-inch skillet, heat the oil over medium-high heat. Add the spinach and green onions and cook, stirring constantly, until the spinach is just wilted, about 1 minute. Remove from the heat and allow to cool slightly.

In a large bowl, stir together the eggs, cream, Tabasco Sauce, and salt until well blended. Stir in the cheese and the spinach mixture.

Unroll the piecrust and use a 3-inch round cookie cutter to cut out 24 rounds. Press a dough round into each muffin cup. Fill each with egg mixture. Bake for 15 minutes or until the mini quiches are golden and puffed.

MAKES 24 MINI QUICHES

Spicy Steak and Eggs Benedict

Perfect for breakfast in bed or a special weekend brunch, this spicy version of a classic will become a go-to recipe.

- 1 1.25-ounce envelope Hollandaise sauce mix (or prepare your favorite Hollandaise sauce from scratch)
- 2 teaspoons Tabasco Pepper Sauce
- 1 tablespoon distilled white vinegar
- 4 large eggs
- 1 tablespoon butter, at room temperature
- 2 English muffins, split
- ½ pound cooked flank steak, thinly sliced

Prepare the Hollandaise sauce according to the package directions, adding 1½ teaspoons of the Tabasco Sauce when you add the water or milk, depending on the brand. (Or stir the Tabasco Sauce into your homemade Hollandaise.) Keep warm.

Fill a large nonstick skillet three-fourths full of water and add the vinegar. Bring to a boil and reduce the heat to low. Break the eggs, one at a time, into a small dish, then slide each egg into the simmering water. Cook for 3 minutes, or until the egg whites turn opaque and the yolks lose their shine. Remove the eggs with a slotted spoon to drain on a plate lined with paper towels.

In a small bowl, blend together the butter and remaining ½ teaspoon Tabasco Sauce. Toast the English muffin halves and spread the butter on them.

To assemble, place 2 English muffin halves on a plate. Top each half with sliced flank steak and a poached egg. Pour Hollandaise over the top and serve immediately.

SERVES 2

Cheese Grits

No Tabasco Sauce cookbook would be complete without a recipe for grits. This one has lots of flavor, so it stands up to our famous Grillades (page 28), and also works nicely with the gravy of any game or chicken dish.

  4   cups chicken broth
  1   cup quick-cooking grits (not instant grits)
1½   cups shredded sharp Cheddar cheese
  1   cup whole milk
  2   large eggs, beaten
  ¾   teaspoon Tabasco Pepper Sauce

Preheat the oven to 350°F. Lightly grease an 11 x 17-inch baking dish.

In a medium saucepan, bring the broth to a boil. Add the grits and cook according to package directions. Remove from the heat and stir in the Cheddar. In a bowl, combine the milk, eggs, and Tabasco Sauce. Stir the milk mixture into the grits. Pour the grits into the baking dish and bake for 30 minutes, until mixture is set.

SERVES 6 TO 8

> **TIP** **TABASCO SAUCE LOVES CHEESE**
> Tabasco Sauce sparks up cheeses of all kinds, bland or sharp. Stir a few drops into cottage cheese and cream cheese dips and spreads; sprinkle it on grilled cheese sandwiches or cheese straws; shake it into fondue, rarebit, quiche, macaroni and cheese, cheese bread, soufflés, cheese balls, cheese soup . . . even add a dash to raclette.

Shirred Eggs with Sherried Mushrooms

One of Cousin Walter's breakfast favorites was shirred eggs with a rasher of bacon. The sherry in the mushrooms gives these eggs a delightfully different flavor, great for brunch accompanied by a spicy Bloody Mary (page 50).

4	tablespoons butter, plus more for the ramekins
¾	pound fresh mushrooms, finely chopped
¾	cup finely chopped onion
1	tablespoon dry sherry
¾	teaspoon Tabasco Pepper Sauce
¼	teaspoon salt
4	thin slices French bread, toasted
8	large eggs
	Chopped fresh parsley, for garnish

Preheat the oven to 350°F.

In a large skillet, heat 2 tablespoons of the butter. Add the mushrooms and onion and cook for 5 minutes, or until tender. Stir in the sherry, Tabasco Sauce, and salt and cook for 1 minute longer.

Spread the toast with the remaining 2 tablespoons butter. Grease four 10-ounce ramekins. Fit a slice of toast into each ramekin and top with a layer of onions and mushrooms. Carefully break 2 eggs into each ramekin. Bake for 15 to 20 minutes, until the eggs are set. Sprinkle with parsley.

SERVES 4

Chicken Hash

Despite its plebeian name, this superb dish is right at home on an elegant table. Here's our version, which is an exceptional way to use up leftover roast chicken.

VELOUTÉ

3	tablespoons butter
1½	cups half-and-half
½	cup chicken broth
3	tablespoons all-purpose flour
½	teaspoon Tabasco Pepper Sauce
	Salt and freshly ground black pepper

HASH

2	tablespoons butter
½	cup finely chopped onion
½	cup finely chopped red or yellow bell pepper
6	ounces mushrooms, thinly sliced
2	tablespoons chopped fresh parsley
	Salt and freshly ground black pepper
2	cups peeled, diced, cooked potatoes
2	cups diced cooked chicken
	Chopped fresh chives

For the velouté: In a small saucepan, melt the butter. In a separate pan, warm the half-and-half and broth. When the butter foams, sprinkle in the flour and cook, stirring, over low heat for 3 minutes. Add the broth mixture, Tabasco Sauce, and salt and pepper to taste. Cook, stirring, for about 2 minutes, or until the sauce thickens. Set the velouté aside.

Position a rack in the top third of the oven and preheat to 400°F. Grease a shallow 2-quart baking dish.

For the hash: In a medium skillet, melt the butter. Add the onion and bell pepper and cook over medium heat until tender, about 10 minutes. Add the mushrooms, parsley, and salt and black pepper to taste. Cook over medium-low heat until all the vegetables are very tender, about 15 minutes. Add the velouté, potatoes, and chicken to the skillet and stir to combine. Transfer the hash to the baking dish and bake for 30 to 40 minutes, or until the hash is bubbling and the top is golden. Sprinkle with chives before serving.

SERVES 4 TO 6

PRESIDENTIAL SEAL OF APPROVAL

Tabasco Sauce has often been a favorite of heads of state and other notables, especially Queen Elizabeth II, who enjoys it in Oeufs Drumkilbo, a lobster and prawn cocktail.

In the 1960s, after one of President Kennedy's weekly White House breakfasts for congressional leaders, House Majority Whip Hale Boggs lamented, "We had serious problems—at breakfast there were no grits, no chicory in the coffee, and no Tabasco Sauce!"

When George H. W. Bush campaigned in 1988, it was predicted that Tabasco Sauce would replace jelly beans as the presidential favorite. A campaign spokesperson characterized Mr. Bush as "a devotee of Tabasco Sauce. He uses Tabasco on his tuna sandwiches and on his eggs." His favorite snack was reported to be fried pork rinds sprinkled with Tabasco Sauce. More recently, the Clinton family is said to be a fan of Tabasco Sauce: President Bill Clinton placed Tabasco on the White House dining table, and former Secretary of State Hillary Clinton used it when traveling on White House business.

Grillades

Grillades is a Southern breakfast specialty that always meets an enthusiastic reception at our table, served with a light, flavorful grits pudding or spoon bread. Grillades should be simmered long enough to be fork-tender, refrigerated overnight, and reheated in the morning. Make them with beef or veal, or try venison, which I cut into julienne strips.

2	pounds boneless beef or veal round steak, cut into 2-inch squares
4	tablespoons vegetable oil
¼	cup all-purpose flour
1	cup chopped onion
1½	cups chopped green bell peppers
2	garlic cloves, minced
1	cup chopped tomatoes
½	teaspoon dried thyme
¾	cup beef broth
½	cup red wine
¾	teaspoon salt
1	bay leaf
1	tablespoon Tabasco Worcestershire Sauce
1½	teaspoons Tabasco Pepper Sauce
3	tablespoons chopped fresh parsley
	Cheese Grits (page 23), for serving

Pound the pieces of meat to ¼ inch thick.

In a Dutch oven or heavy pot, heat 2 tablespoons of the oil. Working in batches, add the meat and brown well, removing each batch to a warm plate.

Add the remaining 2 tablespoons oil and the flour to the pot. Stir over medium heat for about 30 minutes to make a dark brown roux.

Add the onion, bell peppers, and garlic, and cook, stirring often, for about 5 minutes, or until soft. Add the tomatoes and thyme, and cook, stirring, for 3 minutes. Add the broth and wine. Stir well for several minutes, scraping up any bits from the bottom of the pot. Return the meat to the pot and stir in the salt, bay leaf, Tabasco Worcestershire Sauce, and Tabasco Sauce. Reduce the heat and simmer, covered, for 1 hour 30 minutes, or until the meat is very tender, stirring occasionally.

Remove the bay leaf. Stir in the parsley. Let cool, then refrigerate the grillades overnight. Reheat before serving, and serve with cheese grits.

SERVES 6 TO 8

TIP **TABASCO SAUCE AT BREAKFAST**

Tabasco Sauce really wakes up the taste buds. Try it in your favorite pancake batter, stir it into grits, sprinkle it on sausages, shake it on fried or poached eggs. For "hotovers," add ½ teaspoon Tabasco Sauce to the milk called for in your favorite popover recipe.

SOUPS, STARTERS & DRINKS

Peppered Pecans

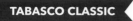

A Louisiana tradition, these spicy pecans are eagerly anticipated by friends visiting our home during the holidays. The slow roasting in a low oven gives them extra crispness. They make a really nice gift, too.

3	tablespoons butter
3	garlic cloves, minced
2½	teaspoons Tabasco Pepper Sauce
½	teaspoon salt
3	cups pecan halves

Preheat the oven to 250°F.

In a small skillet, melt the butter over medium heat. Add the garlic, Tabasco Sauce, and salt and cook for a minute. Toss the pecans with the butter mixture and spread the nuts in a single layer on a baking sheet. Bake for 1 hour, or until the pecans are crisp, stirring occasionally.

MAKES 3 CUPS

> **TIP** For popcorn with zing, shake some Tabasco Sauce into the cooking oil before adding the kernels.

Roasted Red Pepper Dip

A pleasant change from guacamole, this dip has the color and taste to complement crudités, toasted pita bread triangles, or crisp crackers.

> 2   red bell peppers
> 3   slices white bread, crusts removed
> ¼   cup whole milk
> ¼   cup pitted green olives
> 1   garlic clove
> 2   tablespoons olive oil
> 1   tablespoon fresh lemon juice
> ½   teaspoon Tabasco Garlic Pepper Sauce
>   Sliced pitted green olives, for garnish

Preheat the broiler with the rack 3 to 4 inches from the heat.

Halve the peppers lengthwise and pull out the core and seeds. Lay the pieces skin side up on a broiler pan and broil until the skin blisters and turns black. Transfer the peppers to a brown paper bag, close it, and let them steam for 15 minutes. When they are cool enough to handle, peel off the skin.

Meanwhile, break the bread into a small bowl, add the milk, and soak for 10 minutes.

In a food processor, combine the soaked bread, peeled peppers, olives, and garlic and pulse for about 4 seconds. Add the oil, lemon juice, and Tabasco Sauce and pulse 3 seconds longer. Spoon the dip into a serving bowl, cover, and let stand at least 30 minutes to develop the flavors. Garnish with sliced olives.

MAKES 1¼ CUPS

Spicy Spinach and Artichoke Dip

The classic get-together dip gets an upscale makeover with a spicy kick and diced fresh tomatoes.

8   tablespoons (1 stick) butter
1   cup chopped onion
2   10-ounce packages frozen chopped spinach, thawed and well drained
1   14-ounce can artichoke hearts, drained and chopped
8   ounces cream cheese
1   cup sour cream
2   tablespoons Tabasco Pepper Sauce
1   cup shredded Monterey Jack cheese
1   cup grated Parmesan cheese
    Salt
1   cup chopped tomato
    Toasted pita bread wedges, for serving

Preheat the oven to 350°F.

In a large saucepan or skillet, melt the butter over medium heat. Add the onion and cook for 5 minutes, or until soft. Stir in the spinach, artichokes, cream cheese, sour cream, Tabasco Sauce, ¾ cup of the Monterey Jack, ¾ cup of the Parmesan, and salt to taste. Stir until well blended and heated through.

Scrape the mixture into a 1½-quart baking dish and top with remaining ¼ cup Monterey Jack and ¼ cup Parmesan. Bake for 10 minutes, or until the cheeses start to brown. Garnish with tomatoes and serve with pita bread wedges.

MAKES ABOUT 4 CUPS

Guacamole

If you're in a hurry and don't mind a smooth-textured guacamole, make this in a food processor, pulse-chopping the onion first and then adding the rest of the ingredients. By using Tabasco Sauce, there's no need to handle hot peppers, and the degree of hotness can easily be controlled. Serve with tortilla chips or crudités.

2	avocados, halved and pitted
1	small onion, finely chopped
2	tablespoons fresh lime or lemon juice
1	tablespoon Tabasco Green Jalapeño Sauce
½	teaspoon Tabasco Pepper Sauce
½	teaspoon salt

With a spoon, scoop the avocado flesh into a medium bowl and mash with a fork. Add the onion, lime or lemon juice, both Tabasco Sauces, and salt and blend gently but thoroughly. Cover and refrigerate for no more than 1 hour before serving.

MAKES ABOUT 2 CUPS

> **TIP** For a perky crudité dip, combine 1 cup mayonnaise, 1 tablespoon ketchup, and 1 teaspoon Tabasco Sauce and blend well.

Chunky Salsa

Salsa is a staple in our house. We make our own so we can have it as spicy as we like.

- 2 tablespoons olive oil
- 1 cup coarsely chopped onion
- 1 cup coarsely diced green bell pepper
- 1 28-ounce can diced tomatoes
- 1 tablespoon fresh lime juice
- 2 teaspoons Tabasco Pepper Sauce
- ½ teaspoon salt
- 2 tablespoons chopped fresh cilantro or flat-leaf parsley

In a large heavy saucepan, heat the oil over high heat. Add the onion and bell pepper and cook, stirring frequently, for 5 to 6 minutes, or until tender. Add the tomatoes and bring to a boil. Reduce the heat to low and simmer for 6 to 8 minutes, stirring occasionally, until the salsa is slightly thickened. Remove from the heat. Stir in the lime juice, Tabasco Sauce, and salt. Cool to lukewarm, then stir in the cilantro. Spoon the salsa into containers and cover. The salsa keeps in the refrigerator for up to 5 days.

MAKES ABOUT 3½ CUPS

MTK's Sauced Shrimp

Martha Tupper Kay, a special lady from Mississippi, created recipes for McIlhenny Company for many years. She was famous for her shrimp sauce, which has a deliciously complex mix of condiments and spices. If you prefer, the sauce can be served on the side for dipping.

½ cup sour cream

¼ cup mayonnaise

2 tablespoons sweet chili sauce or tomato sauce

1 tablespoon fresh lemon juice

1 tablespoon horseradish

1 teaspoon Tabasco Worcestershire Sauce

½ teaspoon Tabasco Pepper Sauce

1½ teaspoons curry powder

1 tablespoon finely minced mango chutney

2 tablespoons capers, drained

2 pounds shrimp, shelled, deveined, and cooked (at room temperature)

1 tablespoon chopped fresh parsley

In a large bowl, stir together the sour cream, mayonnaise, chili sauce, lemon juice, horseradish, Tabasco Worcestershire Sauce, Tabasco Sauce, curry powder, chutney, and capers. Pour the sauce over the shrimp and toss to coat. Refrigerate for several hours. To serve, mound the shrimp in a serving dish and sprinkle with the parsley and additional capers, if desired.

SERVES 8

Fiery Catfish Fingers

In the South we grow up loving catfish, which is plentiful in the bayous and rivers. Now it's farm grown, and Northerners are discovering its mild and versatile flavor. We coat bite-size fingers of catfish fillets with Tabasco Sauce and deep-fry them for a knock-your-socks-off appetizer. Serve the catfish hot with spicy mayonnaise or picante sauce.

- ½ cup yellow mustard, coarse-ground mustard, or a combination
- 1 egg white, lightly beaten
- 2 teaspoons Tabasco Pepper Sauce
- 1½ pounds catfish fillets, cut into bite-size strips
- ½ cup yellow cornmeal
- ½ cup all-purpose flour
- ½ teaspoon salt
- ¼ teaspoon freshly ground black pepper
- Vegetable oil, for deep-frying (about 1 quart)

In a large bowl, stir together the mustard, egg white, and Tabasco Sauce. Add the fish and toss to coat well. Cover and refrigerate to marinate for 1 hour.

In a shallow dish, mix together the cornmeal, flour, salt, and pepper. Fill a heavy 3-quart saucepan or deep-fryer no more than one-third full with oil and heat over medium heat to 350°F. Dredge the fish in the cornmeal mixture and shake off the excess. Carefully add the fish to the oil, a few pieces at a time. Cook for 2 minutes, or until golden brown and crispy. Drain on paper towels.

SERVES 6 TO 8

Cornmeal Nips

For a change of pace from crackers or rolls, serve these zesty little wafers with soups or salads.

1	cup stone-ground yellow cornmeal
1½	teaspoons sugar
1	teaspoon salt
1	teaspoon grated onion
2	tablespoons butter, melted
1	teaspoon Tabasco Pepper Sauce
1½	cups boiling water
1	large egg, lightly beaten

Preheat the oven to 400°F. Grease a baking sheet.

In a large bowl, mix together the cornmeal, sugar, salt, onion, butter, and Tabasco Sauce. Add the boiling water and stir until it is absorbed. Stir in the egg. Drop by teaspoons onto the baking sheet and bake for 12 to 15 minutes, or until golden. Transfer to a rack to cool.

MAKES 4 DOZEN

> **TIP** Blend up to ½ teaspoon Tabasco Sauce with 1 stick of softened butter to perk up steamed vegetables, breads–just about anything!

Baked Cherrystone Clams with Spicy Butter

When renowned chef Pierre Franey visited Avery Island in 1990, he observed some age-old local commercial enterprises—crawfish farming, oyster shucking, and boudin making—with great curiosity and enthusiasm; in turn, he taught us his secret to delicious cherrystone clams, best enjoyed with a loaf of crusty French bread and a carafe of wine. We Southerners defer to the Yankees on this one.

36 cherrystone clams
½ pound (2 sticks) butter, at room temperature
¼ cup chopped shallots
1 tablespoon chopped garlic
½ teaspoon Tabasco Garlic Pepper Sauce
1 tablespoon Tabasco Worcestershire Sauce
1 tablespoon Dijon mustard
2 tablespoons chopped fresh parsley
2 tablespoons chopped fresh basil
Salt and freshly ground black pepper
French bread, for serving

Preheat the broiler. Open the clams and arrange them neatly on half shells on a baking sheet. In a small bowl, cream the butter with the remaining ingredients. Spoon the mixture evenly over the clams. Place them under the broiler for 1 minute. Serve immediately with French bread.

SERVES 6 TO 8

 TIP A stick of butter melted with ¼ teaspoon Tabasco Sauce makes a super dunk for lobster, clams, artichokes—anywhere plain butter is used.

Portobello Nachos

Even the most devout meat lover will come back for seconds of this rich but waistline-friendly dish.

9 ounces large portobello mushrooms, stems removed, cut into ¼-inch-wide slices

½ cup Tabasco Green Jalapeño Sauce

2 (8-inch) whole wheat tortillas, cut into 6 wedges each

Cooking spray

1 cup canned white beans, such as cannellini beans, rinsed and drained

¼ cup diced red and green bell peppers

1 teaspoon olive oil

¼ cup crumbled cotija cheese (queso añejo)

In a bowl, toss together the mushroom slices and ¼ cup of the Tabasco Sauce. Marinate for 30 minutes.

Meanwhile, preheat the oven to 350°F. Place the tortilla wedges on a baking sheet and coat with cooking spray. Bake for 8 to 10 minutes, or until golden. Set aside, but leave the oven on.

In a food processor, combine the remaining ¼ cup Tabasco Sauce and white beans and process until smooth.

In a 10-inch nonstick skillet over medium-high heat, cook the bell pepper for 5 minutes or until tender, stirring frequently just until tender.

Spread about 1 tablespoon bean purée on each tortilla wedge and top with 1 teaspoon bell pepper. Add some marinated mushrooms to each wedge and sprinkle with 1 tea-spoon cotija cheese. Bake for 5 to 10 minutes, or until lightly browned and the cheese is melted. Serve immediately.

SERVES 2

Hot 'n' Spicy Chicken Wings with Blue Cheese Dip

Here's an easy version of the tangy chicken wings that have captivated people for decades. To make them hotter, just use more Tabasco Sauce. Serve these with plenty of napkins.

DIP

- ½ cup sour cream
- ½ cup mayonnaise
- 2 teaspoons white wine vinegar
- 1 tablespoon chopped fresh parsley
- 1 tablespoon chopped green onions
- ½ teaspoon minced garlic
- 1 tablespoon Tabasco Buffalo Style Hot Sauce
- ½ teaspoon Tabasco Pepper Sauce
- 3 tablespoons crumbled blue cheese
- Salt and freshly ground black pepper

WINGS

- 12 chicken wings
- Vegetable oil, for deep-frying
- 4 tablespoons butter, melted
- 1 teaspoon ketchup
- 1 teaspoon Tabasco Pepper Sauce

- Celery sticks

For the dip: In a bowl, blend together the sour cream, mayonnaise, vinegar, parsley, green onions, garlic, both Tabasco Sauces, blue cheese, and salt and pepper to taste. Set aside.

For the wings: Remove the tips from the wings and discard. Separate the first and second joints of the wings with a sharp knife. Pat the wings dry with paper towels.

Fill a heavy saucepan or deep-fryer with 2 inches oil and heat over medium heat to 350°F. Fry the wings, a few at a time, for about 6 minutes, until golden on all sides. Drain on paper towels.

In a small bowl, mix the melted butter, ketchup, and Tabasco Sauce. Toss the wings in the butter mixture to coat thoroughly. Serve hot, and pass the dip and celery sticks.

MAKES 24 PIECES

A BARRAGE OF BILLBOARDS

In 1890, the year of Grandpère's death, my great-uncle John Avery McIlhenny took over the modest Tabasco Sauce business. He toured the country, meeting the store owners 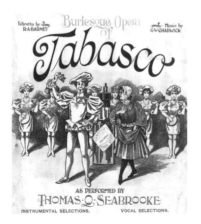 and promoting Tabasco Sauce with a barrage of billboards, demonstrations, giveaways, contests, and even a musical comedy called *The Burlesque Opera of Tabasco*. A veteran of the Rough Riders' Battle for San Juan Heights in Cuba, Uncle John left the company and in 1906 accepted an appointment to the U.S. Civil Service Commission at the behest of his good friend Teddy Roosevelt.

Potato, Artichoke, and Leek Soup

"Elegant" describes this simple creamy soup sparked with Tabasco Sauce. It is superb served in hollowed-out boule bread.

2	tablespoons butter
½	cup chopped onion
1½	cups chopped leeks, white and light green parts only, well washed
1	teaspoon minced garlic
1	quart chicken broth
1	14-ounce can artichoke hearts, drained, rinsed, and quartered
2½	cups peeled, cubed baking potatoes
2	small fresh thyme sprigs
1½	cups whole milk
¾	teaspoon Tabasco Pepper Sauce
	Salt and freshly ground black pepper
	Chopped fresh parsley

In a medium saucepan over medium heat, melt the butter. Add the onion and leeks and cook, covered, for about 10 minutes, or until tender. Uncover and cook until the leeks are very soft, about 5 minutes, adding the garlic at the last minute. Add the broth, artichokes, potatoes, and thyme and simmer for 15 minutes, or until the potatoes are tender. Add the milk and Tabasco Sauce and simmer for 5 minutes longer. Remove from the heat and discard the thyme.

In a food processor or blender, purée the soup until smooth. Season to taste. Serve hot or cold, garnished with parsley.

SERVES 8 TO 10

Oyster Bisque

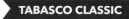

Chilled raw Louisiana oysters and Tabasco Sauce go together like caviar and Champagne. Oysters are great in cooked dishes, too, such as our satisfying bisque.

1 dozen (1 pint) shucked large raw oysters, 1 cup liquor reserved

4 cups whole milk

1 thick onion slice

2 celery stalks, cut into pieces

1 fresh parsley sprig

1 bay leaf

4 tablespoons (½ stick) butter, melted

¼ cup all-purpose flour

½ teaspoon salt

¾ teaspoon Tabasco Pepper Sauce

Chopped fresh chives

Dice the oysters and put them in a saucepan with the reserved liquor. Slowly bring the oysters to a boil over medium-low heat; remove from the heat. In a separate saucepan, combine the milk, onion, celery, parsley, and bay leaf and heat just until steam rises off the milk, then strain out the solids.

In a large saucepan, blend the butter with the flour, salt, and Tabasco Sauce. Slowly stir in the warm milk, and stir over low heat until thickened. Add the oysters and their liquor, and stir for 1 minute, until heated through. Pour into serving bowls and sprinkle with chives.

SERVES 4

> **TIP** Add a finishing dash of Tabasco Sauce to each bowl of oyster stew, clam chowder, or seafood bisque before serving.

Vermilion Bay Fish Chowder

Our Bayou Petite Anse surrounds a good bit of Avery Island and flows into Vermilion Bay, and leads into the Gulf of Mexico. The waters of the bay are home to many species of fish, including the flounder used here, but any white fish can be substituted in this delicious chowder.

  4 tablespoons (½ stick) butter
  ½ cup chopped celery
  ½ cup chopped onion
  ¼ cup all-purpose flour
  2 cups whole milk
  1 8-ounce bottle clam juice
  ½ teaspoon dried basil
  ½ teaspoon dried thyme
  ½ teaspoon salt
  ½ teaspoon Tabasco Pepper Sauce
  1 pound flounder fillets, cut into 1-inch pieces
  2 cups peeled, cubed, and cooked potatoes
  1 15-ounce can whole-kernel corn, undrained

In a 4-quart saucepan, melt the butter over medium heat. Add the celery and onion and cook, stirring frequently, for 5 minutes, or until tender. Stir in the flour and cook for 3 minutes. Gradually stir in the milk and clam juice until smooth. Blend in the basil, thyme, salt, and Tabasco Sauce. Gently stir in the fish, potatoes, and corn, with its liquid. Cook over low heat for 5 minutes, or until the fish flakes easily.

SERVES 6

Red Snapper

This brunch cocktail takes a bit of planning, but the payoff is a comforting tipple with plenty to share.

- 12 pounds tomatoes, cored and coarsely chopped
- 1 (750ml) bottle gin
- 1 tablespoon Tabasco Pepper Sauce, plus more for garnish
- 2 tablespoons Tabasco Worcestershire Sauce
- 1½ tablespoons balsamic vinegar
- 1 tablespoon fresh lime juice
- 2 tablespoons freshly cracked black pepper
- 2 ounces spicy pickle juice
- 2 tablespoons grated fresh horseradish
- 1 16-ounce jar Tabasco Spicy Beans, drained, for garnish
- Cracked white pepper

Process or blend the tomatoes in batches and transfer to a 1-gallon container. Add the remaining ingredients and mix with an immersion blender to a homogeneous state.

Garnish with spicy beans, cracked white pepper, and a dash of Tabasco Sauce.

SERVES 12 TO 16

Classic Bloody Mary

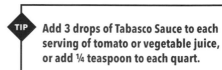

According to legend, the Bloody Mary was created during the 1920s at Harry's New York Bar in Paris. As the cocktail became increasingly popular during the twentieth century, consumers began to regard Tabasco Sauce as an indispensable ingredient. Variations on the Bloody Mary are countless, using ingredients such as clam juice, beef broth, horseradish, garlic, cumin, fresh herbs, coriander, curry powder, soy sauce, barbecue sauce, tequila, aquavit, and even sake.

- 1 quart tomato juice
- 1 cup vodka or gin
- 1 tablespoon fresh lime or lemon juice
- 2 teaspoons Tabasco Worcestershire Sauce
- 1 teaspoon salt
- ¼ teaspoon Tabasco Pepper Sauce, or to taste
  Ice
  Lime slices, celery stalks, or Zydeco Green Beans (page 119), for garnish

Combine all of the ingredients in a 2-quart pitcher. (For a spicier drink, add more Tabasco Sauce.) Stir well and refrigerate until chilled. Serve over ice, garnished with lime slices, celery stalks, or Zydeco Green Beans.

SERVES 6

> **TIP** Add 3 drops of Tabasco Sauce to each serving of tomato or vegetable juice, or add ¼ teaspoon to each quart.

The Morning After

Created by master mixologist Darren Geraghty at The Exchequer gastropub in Dublin, Ireland, this cocktail is fruity, spicy, and citrusy—perfect for the morning after. You can find gingerbread sugar syrup at specialty markets or online.

7	fresh raspberries
1½	ounces vodka
2	tablespoons gingerbread sugar syrup
2	teaspoons fresh lime juice
2	teaspoons fresh lemon juice
¼	teaspoon Tabasco *SWEET & Spicy* Sauce
2	dashes Tabasco Pepper Sauce
	Ice
	Orange zest, for garnish

Muddle the raspberries in the bottom of a cocktail shaker. Add the vodka, sugar syrup, lime juice, lemon juice, and both Tabasco Sauces with ice and shake hard. Strain into a martini glass. Grate orange zest over the drink to garnish.

SERVES 1

Sangrita

This is a drink with spirit–an interesting alternative to the usual brunch offering.

- 1 small onion, peeled and quartered
- 1 cup fresh orange juice
- 4 cups tomato juice
- ⅓ cup fresh lime juice
- 2 tablespoons fresh lemon juice
- 1 teaspoon Tabasco Worcestershire Sauce
- 1 teaspoon sugar
- ½ teaspoon Tabasco Pepper Sauce
- 1¼ cups tequila

  Lime, lemon, and oranges slices, for garnish

In a blender, combine the onion and orange juice and process until smooth. Pour into a 3-quart pitcher. Add the tomato juice, lime juice, lemon juice, Tabasco Worcestershire Sauce, sugar, and Tabasco Sauce. Mix well. Add the tequila and stir. Serve over ice, garnished with lime, lemon, and orange slices.

SERVES 10

> **TIP** For a real kick, create a Cola Volcano by stirring a drop or two of Tabasco Sauce into a cola drink and serving it over ice.

Seeing Red Margaritas

This simple frozen strawberry margarita comes together quickly and can be adjusted for taste by adding more lime juice or sugar.

> 1 cup frozen strawberries
> ⅓ cup tequila
> 2 tablespoons fresh lime juice
> 2 tablespoons superfine sugar
> ½ teaspoon Tabasco Pepper Sauce
> 2 cups ice cubes

In a blender, combine all the ingredients and blend until smooth. Serve immediately.

SERVES 2

Melon Cooler

Sweet honeydew melon meets vodka, lime, and Tabasco Green Jalapeño Sauce in this refreshing cocktail. For a family-friendly version, omit the vodka.

- 4 cups honeydew melon chunks
- 2 tablespoons fresh lime juice
- 1 tablespoon Tabasco Green Jalapeño Sauce
- ½ cup vodka

In a blender or food processor, combine all the ingredients and process until smooth. Chill well.

SERVES 2

THE TABASCO SAUCE TEMPEST

From its beginning, the British have appreciated Tabasco Sauce. In 1874, Grandpère sent his first bottles of Tabasco Sauce to England, and by the end of the decade he had established a permanent presence in the country.

England's love affair with Tabasco Sauce nearly came to an end in 1932. Members of Parliament, fond of French wines and Cuban cigars, were also partial to Tabasco Pepper Sauce, readily available in the House of Commons dining rooms. But when the British Government embarked on an isolationist "Buy British" campaign, Parliament, following suit, banned the purchase of Tabasco Sauce.

The ensuing cries of protest from the MPs were dubbed "The Tabasco Tempest" by amused observers, but generally ignored by the Government. However, "Buy British" inevitably gave way to "Buy Tabasco," and the little bottles of red sauce happily reappeared on parliamentary tables.

MAINS

Autumn Harvest Fettuccine

Butternut squash, leek, red bell pepper, and green beans combine in a festive seasonal dish brimming with flavor.

1	small butternut squash, peeled, seeded, and cut into 1-inch pieces (about 4 cups)
1	leek, sliced and well washed
1	red bell pepper, cut into 1-inch pieces
¼	pound green beans, cut into 2-inch pieces
3	tablespoons olive oil
1½	teaspoons Tabasco Pepper Sauce
1	teaspoon salt
8	ounces fettuccine pasta
¼	cup chopped fresh parsley or basil
¼	cup grated Parmesan cheese

Preheat the oven to 450°F.

Toss together the butternut squash, leek, bell pepper, beans, 2 tablespoons of the oil, 1 teaspoon of the Tabasco Sauce, and ½ teaspoon of the salt in a large roasting pan. Roast for 15 to 20 minutes, stirring occasionally, until the vegetables are browned and tender.

Meanwhile, in a large pot of boiling water, cook the pasta according to package directions. Drain and transfer to a large bowl.

Add the roasted vegetables to the fettuccine along with the parsley and remaining 1 tablespoon oil, ½ teaspoon Tabasco Sauce, and ½ teaspoon salt. Toss together.

Serve with grated Parmesan cheese.

SERVES 4 TO 6

Baked
Mac and Cheese

Our mac and cheese is a simple but tasty adaptation
of the popular pasta dish. Its creamy sauce is a blend of
sharp Cheddar and Gruyère cheeses with a few dashes of
Tabasco Pepper Sauce, which enhances the flavor. For an
added layer of texture, this version is topped with golden
baked bread crumbs.

16	ounces corkscrew or mini penne pasta
4	tablespoons (½ stick) butter
¼	cup all-purpose flour
4	cups whole milk
¾	teaspoon salt
1½	teaspoons Tabasco Pepper Sauce
1	cup shredded Gruyère cheese
1	cup shredded sharp Cheddar cheese

TOPPING

⅓	cup butter
½	cup dried seasoned bread crumbs
½	teaspoon Tabasco Pepper Sauce

Preheat the oven to 375°F.

In a large pot of boiling water, cook the pasta according to
package directions. Drain and set aside.

Meanwhile, in a 3-quart saucepan, melt the butter over
medium heat. Stir in the flour until well blended and smooth.
Gradually whisk in the milk, salt, and Tabasco Sauce. Cook until
thickened and smooth, stirring often. Add the Gruyère and
Cheddar to the sauce and stir until melted. Toss the sauce with
the cooked pasta in a large bowl. Spoon the mixture into an
ungreased 2-quart baking dish.

For the topping: In a small skillet, melt the butter over medium heat. Stir in the bread crumbs and Tabasco Sauce until well blended. Spoon the crumb mixture over the pasta.

Bake for 20 minutes, or until the crumbs are toasted and the mixture is heated through.

SERVES 4 (OR 8 AS A SIDE DISH)

HOST PAR EXCELLENCE

An active member of the exclusive Chevaliers du Tastevin, my cousin Walter McIlhenny loved to entertain and dine well, carrying on the tradition started by Grandpère. He assembled a formidable cookbook collection, and counted among his many friends culinary greats such as Clementine Paddleford, James Beard, and Craig Claiborne. His kitchen was a large square room with a huge, six-by-nine-foot butcher block table dead center, and an array of gleaming copper pots hanging overhead. At his own choosing, his dining table seated no more than eight so each guest could participate in the dinner conversation, and he personally selected the menu and the wines.

Although he built a new pepper sauce plant on Avery Island, introduced modern management and marketing, and expanded sales to more than 100 countries worldwide, Walter resisted pressure to sell the company or change the method of making the sauce. He retained the lengthy quality-minded process from the old family recipe, with its three-year aging period. He always went into the pepper fields to weigh the day's harvest, and personally checked each barrel of aged pepper mash for aroma and color, as well as each batch of finished sauce—a tradition we carry on to this day.

Eula Mae's Cajun Seafood Gumbo

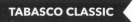

The late Eula Mae Doré is a legend on Avery Island. She retired as proprietor of our Tabasco Deli, where she served wonderful sandwiches and salads to the workers who dropped in for lunch. She and I had a standing dispute over the proper way to cook seafood gumbo. She insisted on Cajun style, which is never made with a roux, while I grew up with the New Orleans roux-based version. Although I disagreed with her method, the result is undeniably delicious.

- ¾ cup vegetable oil
- 2 pounds fresh okra, thinly sliced, or 2 (16-ounce) packages frozen sliced okra, thawed (about 8 cups)
- 1 tablespoon distilled white vinegar
- 4 quarts water
- 2 pounds ham, cubed
- 3 large onions, diced
- 2 celery stalks, diced
- 1 garlic head, cloves peeled but left whole
- 1 green bell pepper, diced
- 1 14.5-ounce can diced tomatoes
- 4 pounds medium shrimp, peeled and deveined
- 2 pounds lump crabmeat
- 1 tablespoon Tabasco Pepper Sauce
- 6 cups cooked rice

In a large skillet (not cast iron), heat ½ cup of the oil over medium heat. Add the okra and cook, stirring frequently, for 30 minutes, or until it is no longer ropy. Add the vinegar and cook, stirring, for another 10 minutes, until the okra takes on a brownish color and is reduced to about a quarter of its original volume. Transfer the okra to a medium bowl and set aside.

In a large stockpot, bring the water to a boil over high heat. Meanwhile, add the remaining ¼ cup oil to the skillet and heat over medium-high heat. Add the ham and cook for about 10 minutes, or until it is lightly browned.

With a slotted spoon, transfer the ham to the stockpot. Add the onions, celery, garlic, and bell pepper to the skillet and cook, stirring constantly, for 10 minutes, until the vegetables are tender. Add the vegetables, okra, and tomatoes to the stockpot. Cover and simmer over medium heat for 1 hour, or until the vegetables are very tender.

Reduce the heat to very low, add the shrimp, and simmer very slowly for 10 minutes. Add the crabmeat and Tabasco Sauce and simmer for an additional 5 to 10 minutes, to blend flavors.

Serve the gumbo in soup bowls with scoops of rice.

SERVES 12 TO 16

GUMBO

Gumbo is a classic Creole or Cajun hearty soup or stew, thickened with okra or *filé*, and served with steamed white rice. If okra is used, it is first cooked in a skillet with a little oil for 30 to 40 minutes, until it loses its slimy ropiness and browns slightly. A teaspoon of vinegar added toward the end of the cooking period helps get rid of the ropiness.

Known as *filé*, powdered sassafras leaves are a gumbo ingredient borrowed from the Choctaw Indians. *Filé* adds seasoning and thickness to a gumbo. Some linguists think the word "gumbo" itself derives from the Choctaw word for *filé* (*kombo ashish*), while others assert it comes from a West African word for "okra" (*guingombo*).

No two gumbos are alike, and they are as good as the cook who makes them.

Chicken and Andouille Gumbo

If you asked a dozen Louisiana cooks for their gumbo recipes, you would get a dozen different ones—providing they agreed to part with their closely guarded family secrets. Gumbos are categorized in many ways: those made with a roux, without a roux, with okra, without okra, with *filé,* etc. There is seafood gumbo, oyster gumbo, gumbo z'herbes, chicken and sausage gumbo, and various combinations thereof. Here is a meat-based version with a full, rich flavor.

6	tablespoons vegetable oil
½	pound andouille or kielbasa sausage, cut into ¼-inch cubes
1	whole chicken (2½ to 3 pounds), cut into serving pieces
1½	quarts water
⅓	cup all-purpose flour
1	cup chopped onion
1	cup chopped celery
1	cup chopped green bell pepper
2	garlic cloves, minced
2	tablespoons chopped fresh parsley
2	bay leaves
½	teaspoon dried thyme
1	teaspoon Tabasco Pepper Sauce
¼	teaspoon salt
⅛	teaspoon freshly ground black pepper
½	cup chopped green onions
2 to 3	cups cooked rice

In a 3-quart saucepan, heat 2 tablespoons of the oil over medium-high heat. Add the sausage and cook for 7 minutes, or until browned. Remove with a slotted spoon and set aside. Add the chicken pieces and cook, turning occasionally, for 10 minutes, or until golden brown. Add the water, cover, and cook for 30 minutes, or until the chicken is tender. Remove the chicken, leaving the liquid in the pan. When the chicken is cool enough to handle, discard the skin and bones and cut the meat into ½-inch chunks.

In a skillet, stir together the remaining 4 tablespoons oil and the flour and cook over medium heat, stirring constantly, for 30 minutes, or until the roux turns dark brown. Add the onion, celery, bell pepper, garlic, and parsley, and cook for 10 minutes, or until the vegetables are tender. Add the vegetables to the liquid in the saucepan, along with the bay leaves, thyme, Tabasco Sauce, salt, and black pepper. Bring to a boil, reduce the heat, and simmer, uncovered, for 45 minutes. Add the chicken and sausage and simmer for another 15 minutes, until tender.

Remove the pan from the heat, add the green onions, and adjust the seasoning. Let the gumbo stand for 10 to 15 minutes. To serve, mound about ⅓ cup rice in each soup bowl, then ladle about 1 cup of gumbo around the rice.

SERVES 6 TO 8

Fred's Hottest Shrimp

Fred Ferretti, a veteran food writer, is rumored to carry a flask of Tabasco Sauce on his hip. He insists this is an exaggeration, but he has been known to shake droplets of the pepper sauce even on dim sum. Here's his recipe for shrimp with a real kick.

1	pound medium shrimp (about 36), peeled and deveined, shells reserved
½	cup water
2	teaspoons Tabasco Pepper Sauce
1	tablespoon ketchup
1	teaspoon salt
1½	teaspoons sugar
	Pinch of white pepper
4	tablespoons olive oil
1	small green bell pepper, cut into ½-inch pieces
1	small red bell pepper, cut into ½-inch pieces
4	garlic cloves, minced
½	cup diced onion
1	tablespoon white wine
	Cooked rice, for serving

In a small saucepan, combine the shrimp shells and water and bring to a boil. Reduce the heat and simmer for 20 minutes. Discard the shells and reserve the stock. In a small bowl, combine 1 tablespoon of the shrimp stock with the Tabasco Sauce, ketchup, salt, sugar, and white pepper and set aside.

In a large skillet, heat 1½ tablespoons of the oil over high heat. When the oil is hot, add the bell peppers and cook for 1 minute. Remove the peppers and set aside. Wipe the pan clean and add the remaining 2½ tablespoons oil and the garlic and onion. Cook over high heat for about 4 minutes, or until the onion is softened and translucent. Stir in the shrimp and cook for 1 minute.

Add the wine and mix well. The shrimp should begin to curl. Add the reserved peppers and stir, cooking for about 30 seconds. Stir the Tabasco Sauce mixture and pour it into the skillet, mixing all ingredients thoroughly. Remove the pan from the heat and transfer the shrimp with the sauce to a warmed serving dish. Serve immediately with cooked rice.

SERVES 4

CAPSICUM, A COLUMBUS DISCOVERY

Tabasco Sauce is made from a variety of pepper called *Capsicum frutescens*, known for centuries in Latin America. The first written reference to a capsicum pepper was made in 1493 by Diego Álvarez Chanca, the physician on Columbus's voyage, who reported that the Indians used a spice called *aji* made from these peppers. Although his search for black pepper was fruitless, Columbus introduced capsicum peppers to the Old World.

A capsicum pepper's personality is determined by a substance called capsaicin, an unusually powerful compound found in no other plant. The capsaicin level in peppers is measured by something called Scoville units, with a hotness range from the mildest bell peppers, with a zero score, to bhut jolokias, or ghost peppers, which rate up to 1.5 million. Scoville units are based on a test, devised by a pharmacologist named Wilbur Scoville, that measures a pepper's perceived "heat" on the human tongue. The *Capsicum frutescens* variety has only a single cultivar in the United States, which is tabasco, and it has a high Scoville score of 30,000 to 50,000. The varietal name of the pepper should not be confused with the trademark Tabasco®.

Shrimp Creole

We love this New Orleans classic spooned over rice, served with crusty bread and a green salad. This is the version we offer to guests, especially those from other areas, as an example of our fine regional cooking.

¼ cup all-purpose flour

1 tablespoon bacon drippings

3 tablespoons vegetable oil

2 cups chopped onion

½ cup chopped green onions

2 garlic cloves, minced

1 cup chopped green bell pepper

1 cup chopped celery, with leaves

1 teaspoon dried thyme

2 bay leaves

2 teaspoons salt

½ teaspoon freshly ground black pepper

1 6-ounce can tomato paste

1 14.5-ounce can diced tomatoes

1 8-ounce can tomato sauce

1 cup fish stock or water

4 pounds medium shrimp, peeled and deveined

1 teaspoon Tabasco Pepper Sauce

½ cup chopped fresh parsley

1 tablespoon fresh lemon juice

2 cups cooked rice

In a Dutch oven or large, heavy pan, stir together the flour, drippings, and oil over medium heat for 30 minutes, or until the roux turns a deep red-brown. Add the onion, green onions, garlic, bell pepper, celery, thyme, bay leaves, salt, and black pepper. Cook, stirring constantly, for 20 minutes, or until the onion is translucent and soft. Stir in the tomato paste and cook for 3 minutes. Add the diced tomatoes, tomato sauce, and stock. Simmer, partially covered, for 1 hour, stirring occasionally.

Add the shrimp and cook for 5 minutes, or until they are just opaque. Stir in the Tabasco Sauce, parsley, and lemon juice. Cover and remove from the heat. This dish is best when allowed to stand for several hours or overnight in the refrigerator. Reheat quickly, without boiling, and serve immediately over rice.

SERVES 8

ROUX

Roux, a mixture of flour and oil or drippings browned slowly over medium heat until the desired color is achieved, is a basic component of Louisiana cooking. It is the starter for many fine Cajun and Creole dishes, contributing color, body, and often a nutty flavor.

To make a roux, melt equal amounts of butter (or oil, shortening, or bacon drippings) and flour in a heavy pot or skillet over medium heat. Stir constantly until the mixture reaches a golden or deeper brown, taking care not to burn it. This can take 20 minutes or more, depending upon the desired darkness of the roux. Don't hurry it. If the mixture burns, discard it and begin again, because even slightly burned roux will ruin a dish. Because the roux will dilute when you stir in the liquid, a good rule of thumb is to make the roux one shade darker than you want the finished dish. According to *Eula Mae's Cajun Kitchen: Cooking Through Seasons on Avery Island*, the shade of roux depends on what you're cooking. She writes, ". . . a lighter roux is preferred for a seafood gumbo so as not to overpower the delicate meat. On the other hand, a darker roux is favored for chicken and sausage, duck and rabbit."

Scallops in Double Pepper Sauce

Slivers of red and green bell peppers give this quickly prepared dish vibrant color, and the garlic, Tabasco Sauce, and capers provide lots of flavor.

- ¼ cup olive oil
- 3 garlic cloves, coarsely chopped
- 1 pound bay (whole) or sea (halved or quartered) scallops
- ¾ cup slivered red bell peppers
- ¾ cup slivered green bell peppers
- ½ cup chopped onion
- 1 teaspoon Tabasco Garlic Pepper Sauce
- ¼ teaspoon salt
- 2 tablespoons drained capers

In a large skillet, heat the oil over medium heat. Add the garlic and cook for 1 minute, or until golden. Add the scallops, bell peppers, onion, Tabasco Sauce, and salt. Cook, stirring constantly, for 5 minutes, or just until the scallops turn white and the vegetables are crisp-tender. Stir in the capers and serve immediately.

SERVES 4

> **TIP**
>
> **TABASCO SAUCE AND SEAFOOD**
> Tabasco Sauce is the perfect partner for all sorts of seafood. Sprinkle it on sautéed soft-shell crabs, pan-fried trout or shad roe, grilled fish, boiled crabs or shrimp, clam fritters, seviche, clams casino, and oysters Rockefeller. For more delicate-flavored fish and seafood, mix Tabasco Sauce with melted butter or add it to cocktail sauce. The exception is oysters, which revel in the red stuff.

Dressed Seafood Po' boys

The po' boy is a New Orleans classic and can be made with any type of filling, from roast beef to shrimp to sausage to catfish. What makes a po' boy is the bread—a French bread with a crusty outside and soft, fluffy interior can't be beat. A "dressed" po' boy will have lettuce, tomato, pickles, and mayonnaise.

1   cup mayonnaise
1   garlic clove, crushed through a press
2½ teaspoons Tabasco Pepper Sauce
1   (24-inch) loaf French bread, cut into 4 pieces, or 4 (6-inch) hero rolls
    Oil, for deep-frying
1   large egg
¼ cup whole milk
¾ cup cornmeal
¾ cup all-purpose flour
    Salt
1   pound medium shrimp, peeled and deveined, or 3 dozen shucked oysters
2   cups shredded lettuce
1   tomato, thinly sliced

In a small bowl, combine the mayonnaise, garlic, and 1½ teaspoons of the Tabasco Sauce. Split the French bread or rolls in half. Scoop out some of the soft insides and discard. Spread the insides of the bread halves with the mayonnaise mixture.

Fill a heavy saucepan or deep-fryer with 3 inches oil and heat over medium heat to 375°F.

Meanwhile, in a small bowl, beat together the egg and milk.

In a shallow pan, combine the cornmeal, flour, and ½ teaspoon salt. Sprinkle the shrimp with salt to taste and the remaining 1 teaspoon Tabasco Sauce and toss well.

Dip the shrimp in the egg mixture, then coat with the cornmeal mixture. Shake off excess coating and fry in batches for 3 minutes, or until golden brown. (If using oysters, fry for 1 to 2 minutes.) Drain on paper towels.

Fill the bottom halves of the bread with hot shrimp and top with the lettuce, tomato, and the top of the bread. Serve immediately.

SERVES 4

TABASCO SAUCE CAPTURES THE WORLD

Tabasco Sauce is labeled in twenty-two languages and dialects for shipment to more than 160 countries and territories.

After the United States, Japan consumes more Tabasco Sauce than any other country. The Japanese splash it on pizza and spaghetti. In Belgium it is always included in *filet américain* (steak tartare). In Israel, it is used most frequently on the ubiquitous falafel. Oil workers brought it to the United Arab Emirates, where it is popular in tabbouleh and sambossa.

In Italy, hot pepper seasoning has been adopted by southern Italians as an alternative to expensive Eastern spices. Italians find it a good combination with olive oil. In France, Tabasco Sauce is found mostly in urban centers like Paris, and used in tomato juice and steak tartare. In Canada, the favorite use is in the Bloody Caesar, a tomato and clam juice drink. Australians put it in potent drinks with names like Rambo, Rocky, and Dirty Harry.

Tabasco is also popular in Sweden and the Netherlands, where the basic, mellower seasonings such as salt and pepper, cinnamon, ginger, allspice, and bay leaf gave way to hotter, spicier tastes.

Judy McIlhenny's Crawfish Étouffée

Although fresh crawfish have limited availability outside of the South, we would be remiss not to include at least one beloved "mudbug" recipe. Because crawfish are farmed in Louisiana, they can be obtained precooked and peeled. My wife's recipe for crawfish étouffée is simple and unembellished, allowing the wonderful taste of the crawfish to come through. You can order crawfish from the mail-order companies listed on page 141.

½ pound (2 sticks) butter
1½ cups chopped onion
1 cup chopped green bell pepper
1 cup chopped celery
3 garlic cloves, minced
1 teaspoon salt, or to taste
1 teaspoon Tabasco Pepper Sauce
2 tablespoons crawfish fat (see Note)
2 pounds peeled crawfish tails (about 6 to 7 pounds in the shell)
Juice of ½ lemon
½ cup chopped fresh parsley
½ cup chopped green onions, green part only
Cooked rice, for serving

In a Dutch oven or large heavy pot, melt the butter over medium heat. Add the onion, bell pepper, celery, and garlic and cook for 5 minutes, or until soft. Add the salt, Tabasco Sauce, and crawfish fat, and cook, uncovered, over medium-low heat for 30 minutes, stirring occasionally. Add the crawfish tails, lemon juice, and parsley. Cook for 1 minute, then remove from heat and let sit, covered, for 10 minutes. Just before serving, add the chopped green onions.

For the best flavor, prepare this dish the day before. Remove from the refrigerator 1 hour before serving, and reheat just until hot to avoid overcooking the crawfish. Serve over white rice.

SERVES 6 TO 8

Note: If you cannot purchase crawfish fat separately, you can extract it from the crawfish by running the sealed package of tails under hot water to make the fat more liquid. Cut open the package and empty it into a sieve with a bowl underneath to catch the fat that runs off.

CRAWFISH

The famous mudbugs of Louisiana, crawfish (*écrevisses*) are in season for about six months of the year, from December to June. The rest of the time they burrow six or more feet under the damp soil of the Louisiana wetlands. Resembling miniature lobsters, these tiny crustaceans weigh only an ounce or so, and their tails are delicious in bisque, gumbo, and étouffée, and especially deep-fried (Cajun popcorn). A seasonal Louisiana tradition is whole crawfish boiled in a peppery broth along with corn, whole onions, and unpeeled potatoes, and served up in quantity with plenty of paper napkins. An experienced crawfish eater will quickly pinch the tail meat out of the shell and suck the body cavity, or "head."

Frog Legs Piquant

Nothing's more fun and mysterious than going frog
hunting on a dark, hot, humid summer night in Miss
Sadie's pond, a stone's throw behind my place, which we
call Froggy Bottom because of its proximity to the pond.
The legs of the bullfrogs on Avery Island can be as big
as chicken drumsticks, and they are outstanding fare. We
figure on two or three per person. If you can't get frog
legs, simply substitute catfish or chicken (see Note).

2	tablespoons vegetable oil
4	tablespoons all-purpose flour
3	tablespoons butter
1	large onion, diced
1	celery stalk, diced
½	green bell pepper, diced
3	garlic cloves, minced
1	6-ounce can tomato paste
1	14.5-ounce can diced tomatoes
4	cups chicken broth
1	teaspoon Tabasco Pepper Sauce
½	teaspoon Tabasco Worcestershire Sauce
½	teaspoon freshly ground black pepper
3	pounds large frog legs (15 to 20)
	Salt
	Cayenne pepper
	Cooking spray
	Cooked rice, for serving

In a large saucepan, combine the oil and 2 tablespoons of the
flour to make a roux and cook over medium-high heat, stirring
constantly, for about 15 minutes, or until it is light to medium

brown. Stir in the butter. Add the onion, celery, bell pepper, and garlic, and cook, stirring, for about 5 minutes, or until soft. Add the tomato paste and cook over medium heat for about 10 minutes, stirring frequently. Add the diced tomatoes, broth, Tabasco Sauce, Tabasco Worcestershire Sauce, and black pepper. Cover and simmer over low heat for 45 minutes until flavors develop, stirring occasionally.

Meanwhile, season the remaining 2 tablespoons flour with a small amount of salt and cayenne pepper. Dust the frog legs with the seasoned flour. Coat a large skillet with cooking spray or a small amount of oil over medium-high heat. Add the frog legs and cook for about 3 minutes per side, or until lightly browned all over.

Add the legs to the sauce and simmer, covered, for an additional 15 minutes until frog legs are cooked and tender. Serve over steamed rice.

SERVES 6

Note: If using cut-up chicken, brown the pieces 5 to 10 minutes longer, until nearly cooked through, and simmer in the sauce for 25 minutes. If using catfish fillets, add directly to the sauce and simmer for 20 minutes.

Hot Grilled Trout

Charcoal-grilled fish takes on a new level of flavor when marinated in this wonderful sauce, intensified by a full tablespoon of Tabasco Sauce.

¼ cup fresh lemon juice
2 tablespoons olive oil
2 tablespoons vegetable oil
2 tablespoons chopped fresh parsley
2 tablespoons sesame seeds
1 tablespoon Tabasco Pepper Sauce
1 teaspoon grated fresh ginger
½ teaspoon salt
4 whole brook trout (about 1 pound each), cleaned

In a shallow dish (large enough to hold the trout), mix together the lemon juice, olive oil, vegetable oil, parsley, sesame seeds, Tabasco Sauce, ginger, and salt. With a fork, pierce the skin of each fish in several places. Roll the fish in the lemon juice mixture to coat thoroughly. Leave the fish in the marinade, cover the dish, and refrigerate for 30 minutes to 1 hour, turning the fish occasionally.

Prepare a charcoal fire, or preheat gas grill for grilling.

Remove the fish, reserving the marinade, and place them in a hand-held hinged grill basket. Brush the fish with the marinade. Cook about 4 inches from the hot coals for 5 minutes. Turn, brush with marinade, and cook for 5 minutes longer, or until the flesh appears opaque and flakes easily.

TIP For a fat-free sauce for grilled fish or chicken, purée roasted and peeled red bell pepper, and for every cup add ¼ teaspoon Tabasco Sauce.

SERVES 4

Salmon Steaks with Cucumber Sauce

Tabasco Sauce nicely sparks this simple recipe for broiled salmon steaks, with a contrasting cool sour cream and cucumber sauce.

1 cup sour cream
½ teaspoon Tabasco Pepper Sauce
1 cup seeded and diced unpeeled cucumber
¼ teaspoon salt
1 tablespoon minced fresh dill
4 tablespoons (½ stick) butter, melted
4½ teaspoons fresh lime or lemon juice
4 salmon steaks (6 to 8 ounces each, 1 inch thick)
Salt
Lemon slices, for garnish

In a medium bowl, blend together the sour cream and ¼ teaspoon of the Tabasco Sauce. Stir in the cucumber, salt, and dill. Set aside.

Position a rack 4 inches from the heat and preheat the broiler.

In a small bowl, combine the melted butter, lime juice, and remaining ¼ teaspoon Tabasco Sauce. Place the salmon steaks on a greased broiler pan. Sprinkle them lightly with salt and drizzle on the butter mixture. Broil for 5 minutes per side, or until the flesh appears opaque.

Serve garnished with lemon slices, with the sauce on the side.

SERVES 4

Eula Mae's Jambalaya

Jambalaya is a Spanish-Creole one-pot meal made with rice and whatever is on hand—shrimp, chicken, oysters, sausage, crabs, cowpeas, or turkey. Everyone has their own version, and this recipe came from the late Eula Mae Doré, a longtime Avery Island resident known for her excellent Cajun cooking. She said that scraping up all the browned bits from the bottom of the pot gave her jambalaya its special color and flavor.

1	whole chicken (3 pounds), boned and skinned and cut into bite-size chunks, or 1½ pounds boneless, skinless breasts and thighs, cut into 1-inch cubes
1	teaspoon salt
⅛	teaspoon freshly ground black pepper
⅛	teaspoon cayenne pepper
2	tablespoons vegetable oil
½	pound ham, cut into ½-inch cubes
2	large onions, chopped
1	medium green bell pepper, chopped
1	cup chopped celery
4	garlic cloves, peeled but whole
3	cups chicken broth
1	14.5-ounce can whole tomatoes, drained and chopped, juice reserved
2	tablespoons chopped fresh parsley
½	cup chopped green onions
2	pounds medium shrimp, peeled and deveined
1	teaspoon Tabasco Pepper Sauce
2	cups raw long-grain white rice, rinsed and drained

Sprinkle the chicken cubes with the salt, black pepper, and cayenne. In a large heavy pot or Dutch oven, heat the oil over medium heat. Add the chicken and cook, stirring, for 8 to 10 minutes, or until browned on all sides. Transfer the chicken to a bowl. Add the ham to the pot and cook for about 5 minutes, or until lightly browned, then add it to the chicken.

Add the onions, bell pepper, celery, and garlic in the pot and cook for about 5 minutes, scraping up any browned bits from the bottom of the pan. Return the chicken and ham to the pan, reduce the heat to low, cover, and cook for 25 minutes, stirring occasionally. Add the broth and reserved tomato juices to the pot, cover, and simmer for 45 minutes to blend flavors.

Mash the cooked garlic against the side of the pan and stir into the mixture. Add the tomatoes, parsley, green onions, shrimp, and Tabasco Sauce, and adjust the seasoning to taste. Add the rice. Bring to a boil, reduce the heat, cover, and simmer, stirring occasionally, for 25 to 30 minutes, or until the rice is tender and fluffy and the liquid is absorbed.

SERVES 6 TO 8

JAMBALAYA

According to some sources, jambalaya is derived from *jambon*, the French word for ham, and *alaya*, which means rice in an African dialect. This dish is a wonderful conglomeration of sausages, chicken, ham, and seafood cooked with rice. It is a Louisiana tradition, favored by Cajuns and Creoles alike. The rice absorbs all the flavors of the basic seasonings, which include onions, bell peppers, tomatoes, garlic, herbs, green onions, and, of course, Tabasco Sauce. The variations are infinite, and they're all delicious.

Chicken Olé Mole

Mexico, the assumed birthplace of our special hot peppers, is also home to more mole sauces than one can count. This simplified version uses Tabasco Sauce in place of chiles.

2	tablespoons olive oil
1	whole chicken (2 to 3 pounds), cut into pieces
½	cup finely chopped onion
½	cup finely chopped green bell pepper
1	small garlic clove, minced
¼	cup slivered almonds
¼	cup raisins
1½	tablespoons toasted sesame seeds
½ to 1	cup chicken broth
1	8-ounce can tomato sauce
1½	ounces unsweetened chocolate, coarsely chopped
1	teaspoon Tabasco Pepper Sauce
½	teaspoon Tabasco Chipotle Sauce
½	teaspoon ground cinnamon
¼	teaspoon ground allspice

In a large skillet, heat 1 tablespoon of the oil over medium heat. Add the chicken pieces and brown all over. Remove and set aside. Add the remaining 1 tablespoon oil to the skillet. Add the onion, bell pepper, and garlic and cook for 3 to 5 minutes, until crisp-tender.

In a food processor or blender, finely grind the almonds, raisins, and sesame seeds to a paste. Add the mixture to the vegetables in the skillet, along with ½ cup of the broth, the tomato sauce, chocolate, both Tabasco Sauces, cinnamon, and allspice. Cook, stirring, until the chocolate melts.

Return the chicken to the skillet, coating the pieces well with the sauce. If the sauce is too thick, add a little more broth, about ½ cup. Cover and simmer over low heat for 30 to 40 minutes, or until the chicken is cooked through.

SERVES 4

RARE DUCK

My father insisted that the only way to eat wild duck breasts was rare, and his recipe was simple: "Have a slow-gaited butler walk it on a platter through a hot kitchen."

For the finer-tasting wild ducks, like teal, pintail, wood duck, mallard, and ringneck, cooking them rare to medium-rare is just right. To prepare duck breasts, with a sharp boning knife cut close to the breastbone on each side of the duck and remove the breasts. Dip each breast in melted butter, and cook in a hot skillet over high heat for 3½ minutes per side. For larger ducks like the mallard, slice the uncooked breasts thinly across the grain, then salt and pepper them lightly and cook for 4½ minutes on each side. Cover the slices with muscadine jelly. Serve with wild rice on the side. Use the carcasses to make duck and andouille gumbo.

Fried Chicken

In the South, everyone has a tried-and-true way to make fried chicken. Some will serve it with Tabasco on the side, while others are gravy purists. Our fried chicken has the right amount of spicy bite with a crispy crunch.

3 cups buttermilk
¼ cup Tabasco Pepper Sauce
3 teaspoons salt
1 whole chicken (2½ to 3 pounds), cut into 8 pieces
2 cups all-purpose flour
1 teaspoon garlic powder
½ teaspoon onion powder
¼ teaspoon freshly ground black pepper
    Canola oil, for deep-frying

In a large bowl or large resealable plastic bag, combine the buttermilk, Tabasco Sauce, and 1 teaspoon of the salt and mix well. Add the chicken and cover the bowl or seal the bag. Refrigerate for at least 6 and up to 24 hours.

In a shallow dish, combine the flour, garlic powder, onion powder, pepper, and remaining 2 teaspoons salt. Remove the chicken pieces from the marinade and allow the excess buttermilk to drip off. Dredge the chicken pieces in the seasoned flour and let the chicken sit for 10 minutes.

Fill a large, deep skillet with 1 inch oil and heat over medium-high heat to 350°F.

Working in batches of 4 pieces, fry the chicken, turning occasionally, for 10 minutes per side, or until golden brown and cooked through. Transfer the chicken to a rack set on a baking sheet.

SERVES 4

Individual Sugar Snap Pea and Chicken Pot Pies

Untraditional but delicious, these shortcut chicken pot pies look spectacular with their puff pastry bonnets. They are a great way to use up leftover roast chicken.

2½ cups chicken broth

1 baking potato, peeled and cut into ½-inch cubes

1½ cups carrot slices (½ inch thick)

1 cup frozen pearl onions

½ teaspoon dried rosemary

2 teaspoons Tabasco Green Jalapeño Sauce

¼ teaspoon salt

1 red bell pepper, coarsely diced

¼ pound (about 1 cup) sugar snap peas, trimmed and halved lengthwise

3 tablespoons butter, plus more for the ramekins

¼ cup all-purpose flour

8 ounces cooked chicken breast, cut into 1 x 3-inch strips

1 sheet frozen puff pastry, thawed

1 egg, beaten with 1 teaspoon water

In a large, heavy saucepan, bring the broth to a boil over high heat. Add the potato, carrots, onions, rosemary, Tabasco Sauce, and salt. Reduce the heat to medium, cover, and simmer for 8 to 10 minutes, or until the vegetables are tender. Add the bell pepper and peas and boil for 30 seconds, just until the peas turn bright green. Drain the vegetables in a colander set over a bowl to catch the chicken broth. Set aside.

In a saucepan, melt the butter over low heat. Stir in the flour and cook for 3 to 4 minutes, stirring constantly. Pour in 2 cups of the reserved chicken broth and whisk until smooth. Bring to a boil over medium heat, stirring constantly. Reduce the heat to low and simmer for 5 minutes, until thickened and bubbling, stirring frequently.

Preheat the oven to 475°F. Lightly butter four 10-ounce ramekins or soufflé dishes.

Put the chicken strips in the bottoms of the ramekins or soufflé dishes. Top the chicken with the vegetables. Divide the sauce evenly among the ramekins. On a floured surface, cut 4 rectangles slightly larger than the ramekins. You will have leftover pastry. Brush the outside of the ramekin rims with some of the beaten egg mixture. Place a pastry rectangle over each ramekin and press firmly around the edges to seal. Trim the dough to make a neat edge and brush the tops with the egg mixture. Put the ramekins on a baking sheet and bake for 10 to 12 minutes, until the pastry is puffed and well browned. Serve at once.

SERVES 4

The second Tabasco factory (1905–1980) is now part of our corporate office on Avery Island.

Peppery Sausage and Onion Grilled Pizza

Sweet sausage and onions combine with Tabasco Sauce for a surprisingly complex-tasting grilled pizza.

- 1 pound sweet Italian sausage
- 1 sweet onion, cut into ½-inch-thick slices
- 1 green bell pepper, cut into ½-inch-wide slices
- 1 tablespoon olive oil
- 2 teaspoons Tabasco *SWEET & Spicy* Sauce
- 1 tablespoon Tabasco Pepper Sauce
- 1 garlic clove, crushed through a press
  All-purpose flour, for rolling
- 1 pound prepared pizza dough
- ½ cup shredded mozzarella cheese

Preheat a grill to medium-high.

Grill the sausage, onion, and pepper slices until the sausage is no longer pink. When the sausage is cool, cut into ¼-inch-thick slices. In a bowl, combine the oil, both Tabasco Sauces, and garlic.

On floured surface with a floured rolling pin, roll the dough into two 10-inch rounds about ¼ inch thick. Carefully place the dough rounds on the grill. Cover the grill; the dough will puff slightly in 2 to 3 minutes. Immediately flip the dough onto the coolest part of the grill. Quickly brush the grilled surface of the dough with the oil mixture. Top with the sausage, peppers, onion, and mozzarella. Slide the pizzas back over direct heat and grill, rotating them often so they don't burn, about 5 minutes. Pizzas are done when the crust is crisp, the tops are bubbling, and the cheese is slightly melted. Serve immediately.

MAKES 2 PIZZAS/SERVES 4

The Ultimate Hamburger

The late Craig Claiborne, cookbook author and former food editor of the *New York Times*, was a great longtime friend and Tabasco Sauce fan. He said Tabasco Sauce was "absolutely essential" for this hamburger.

1½ pounds ground round steak
    Salt and freshly ground black pepper
4 tablespoons (½ stick) butter
1 teaspoon Tabasco Worcestershire Sauce
½ teaspoon Tabasco Pepper Sauce, or to taste
    Juice of ½ lemon
4 hamburger buns or 8 slices whole wheat bread, toasted
⅓ cup finely chopped fresh parsley

Divide the meat into 4 portions and shape each into a round patty. Handle the meat lightly, pressing just enough so that it holds together.

Sprinkle the bottom of a very heavy skillet, preferably cast iron, with a very light layer of salt, and heat the skillet until it is searingly hot. Add the patties and sear well on each side. Using a pancake turner, quickly turn the patties and reduce the heat. Cook the patties to the desired degree of doneness, 3 minutes or longer. When the hamburgers are done, sprinkle them with salt and pepper to taste and top each with 1 tablespoon butter. Sprinkle on the Tabasco Worcestershire Sauce, Tabasco Sauce, and lemon juice.

Transfer each hamburger to the bottom of a hamburger bun or slice of toast. Sprinkle with parsley. Add the top of the bun or another slice of toast.

SERVES 4

Walter's Chili

My cousin, the late Walter McIlhenny, was very fond of homemade chili and liked to serve his version to former Marine Corps buddies who visited him on the Island.

¼ cup vegetable oil

3 pounds lean beef chuck, well trimmed, cut into 1-inch cubes

1 cup chopped onion

3 garlic cloves, minced

3 tablespoons chili powder

2 teaspoons ground cumin

2 teaspoons salt

1½ teaspoons Tabasco Habanero Sauce

3 cups water

1 4-ounce can chopped green chiles, drained

Cooked rice, for serving

Chopped onion, shredded Cheddar or Monterey Jack cheese, and sour cream (optional)

In a 5-quart Dutch oven or heavy saucepan, heat the oil over medium-high heat. In three batches, brown the beef well, removing each batch with a slotted spoon. Set aside.

Add the onion and garlic to the pot and cook, stirring frequently, for 5 minutes, or until tender. Stir in the chili powder, cumin, salt, and Tabasco Habanero Sauce and cook for 1 minute. Add the water and chiles and bring to a boil. Return the beef to the pot. Reduce the heat and simmer, uncovered, for 1 hour 30 minutes, or until the beef is tender.

Serve the chili over rice garnished with onion, cheese, and sour cream, if desired.

SERVES 4 TO 6

Perfect Seared Steaks

This is our favorite way to cook steaks outdoors on a charcoal grill, and it works well with hamburgers too. Start with a good "steak fire" of white coals 3 to 4 inches below the grill. To test the fire, put the palm of your hand just above the grill. If you can keep it there only for as long as it takes to say "one thousand and one," the fire is ready.

4	bone-in New York strip or rib-eye steaks, 2 inches thick
2 to 3	teaspoons Tabasco Pepper Sauce
	Freshly cracked black pepper
	Salt

Prepare a charcoal grill for a good "steak fire" (or preheat the broiler with the rack 6 inches from the heat).

With the back of a spoon, briskly rub each side of the steaks with about ¼ teaspoon Tabasco Sauce and some black pepper.

Grill the steaks over direct heat for about 5 minutes on each side for medium-rare; or broil (on an oiled broiler rack) for 4 to 5 minutes on each side for medium-rare. Season with salt to taste. Let steak stand for 5 minutes before serving.

SERVES 4

Sweet and Smoky Baby Back Ribs

The deep smoky flavor of Tabasco Chipotle Pepper Sauce takes classic ribs from an all-day smoking affair to a quick backyard BBQ staple.

2 racks baby back ribs (about 3 pounds)

MARINADE

¼ cup apple cider

2 tablespoons light brown sugar

2 tablespoons fresh lemon juice

2 tablespoons Tabasco Chipotle Pepper Sauce

RUB

1 tablespoon paprika

1 tablespoon light brown sugar

1 teaspoon salt

1 teaspoon garlic powder

½ teaspoon onion powder

2 tablespoons Tabasco Chipotle Pepper Sauce

GLAZE

¼ cup ketchup

Trim the ribs.

For the marinade: In a medium bowl or a large resealable plastic bag, combine the cider, brown sugar, lemon juice, and Tabasco Sauce. Add the ribs and turn to coat with the marinade. Cover (or seal) and refrigerate for at least 2 hours and up to overnight, turning occasionally.

For the rub: In a small bowl, combine the paprika, brown sugar, salt, garlic powder, onion powder, and Tabasco Sauce.

Remove the ribs from the marinade and blot dry with paper towels. Spread the rub mixture on both sides of the ribs.

Preheat a grill to medium-low. Grill the ribs, covered, for 45 minutes, turning occasionally. During the last 10 minutes of grilling, brush the ribs with the ketchup glaze.

SERVES 4

CHEERING UP THE MILITARY

Since at least as early as 1888, when a British soldier in the Himalayan foothills of India wrote home about how Tabasco Sauce improved his meals, our fiery product has been appreciated by the military. My cousin, Walter Stauffer McIlhenny, who was affectionately nicknamed "Tabasco Mac," came up with the *Charlie Ration Cookbook*, or *No Food Is Too Good for the Man up Front* to help U.S. troops in Vietnam make their rations taste better. The recipes showed soldiers how to spice up their C-rations with Tabasco Sauce to create dishes like Battlefield Fufu and Combat Zone Burgoo, also injecting a little humor into otherwise grim eating conditions.

Thousands of copies went to soldiers, wrapped around two-ounce bottles of Tabasco Sauce in special waterproof canisters. When field rations changed, he published a new booklet using the updated "Meal, Ready-to-Eat" (MRE) rations, and during Desert Shield and Desert Storm, Tabasco Sauce miniatures were included in every third MRE packet sent to troops in the Gulf. Hundreds of them wrote to say "Thanks."

In a letter dated July 31, 1991, General H. Norman Schwarzkopf wrote, "Your product has always been in demand by troops in the field. I have enjoyed spicing up my own rations with your pepper sauce for many years. During Operation Desert Shield and Desert Storm the young service men and women appreciated any touch of home and your product was certainly among the most sought after." Miniature bottles of Tabasco Sauce went on to liven up rations during Operation Iraqi Freedom and Operation Enduring Freedom, and they remain in U.S. rations to this day.

Gingered Pork Roast

Cajuns love roast pork. A favorite way to cook it is in a "Cajun microwave" (such as those sold under the brand name Caja China), a large wooden box with a metal pan as a cover. The recipe calls for a 100-pound pig, 20 pounds of charcoal, and a case of beer. The pig goes in the box, the charcoal is heaped on top in the pan, and the beer goes into the cook.

An easier and quite delicious version is this smaller pork loin roast, infused with ginger, garlic, sage, and Tabasco Sauce, often the centerpiece of holiday meals in our home. The puréed vegetables make a light and flavorful gravy.

1	tablespoon minced fresh ginger
2	garlic cloves, minced
1	teaspoon dried sage
½	teaspoon salt
1	5-pound pork loin roast
½	cup Tabasco Pepper Jelly, melted
1	teaspoon Tabasco Pepper Sauce
2	medium carrots, cut into ½-inch slices
2	medium onions, cut into ½-inch slices
1¾	cups water

Preheat the oven to 325°F.

In a small dish, combine the ginger, garlic, sage, and salt. Rub the mixture over the pork. Place the meat in a shallow roasting pan and roast for 1 hour 30 minutes. Remove from the oven, then score the top of the roast in a diamond pattern.

In a small bowl, mix together the melted Tabasco Pepper Jelly and Tabasco Sauce, and spread it generously over the roast. Arrange the carrots and onions around the meat, then add 1 cup of the water. Roast up to 1 hour longer, or until a meat thermometer registers 145°F. Remove the roast to a serving platter and keep warm.

Skim the fat from the pan drippings, then purée the cooked vegetables and pan liquids in a food processor or blender. Transfer the purée to a saucepan and stir in the remaining ¾ cup water. Reheat the gravy and serve with the roast.

SERVES 6 TO 8

CAJUN OR CREOLE?

The word *Cajun* refers to the descendants of Acadian exiles from Nova Scotia and other ethnic groups with whom these exiles intermarried on the south Louisiana frontier. *Creole,* on the other hand, is a complex word with several meanings in "the Bayou State" and beyond. When applied to cuisine, however, *Cajun,* according to the *Encyclopedia of Louisiana,* is "associated with rural or small-town fare centered around a single course;" while *Creole* "is strongly associated with New Orleans, where the term suggests urbane, multi-course dining." Both styles of Louisiana cuisine draw heavily on French, Spanish, Acadian, Native American, and Afro-Caribbean influences.

Jalapeño Pork Tacos with Pineapple Salsa and Pickled Onion

These irresistible tacos are both sweet and spicy. In place of pork, try boneless, skinless chicken breasts.

- 1 pork tenderloin (about 1¼ pounds)
- 1 tablespoon plus 2 teaspoons Tabasco Green Jalapeño Sauce
- 1 red onion, thinly sliced
- 1½ cups red wine vinegar
- 3 cups diced fresh pineapple
- ½ teaspoon salt
- ¼ teaspoon freshly ground black pepper
- 8 corn tortillas, heated

Rub the pork with 1 tablespoon of the Tabasco Sauce and refrigerate for at least 1 hour.

In a glass bowl, combine the onion and vinegar. Set aside for 25 minutes and then drain.

In a bowl, combine the pineapple and the remaining 2 teaspoons Tabasco Sauce and set the salsa aside.

Preheat a grill to medium-high heat. Sprinkle the pork with the salt and pepper and grill for about 15 minutes, or until the desired doneness, turning once. Let pork sit for 5 minutes before slicing.

In a 12-inch skillet over medium-high heat, heat a few tortillas at a time until lightly browned, turning once. Or, wrap tortillas in damp paper towels and microwave for 1 to 2 minutes until hot. Top with sliced pork, pineapple salsa, and pickled onions.

SERVES 4

Pepper-Stuffed Lamb with Garlic Chèvre Sauce

This is exceptional dinner party fare: impressive looking and superb tasting, flavored with herbs, sun-dried tomatoes, Tabasco Sauce, garlic, and goat cheese.

LAMB

- 2 red or green bell peppers
- 1 leg of lamb (6 to 7 pounds), boned and butterflied
  Salt and freshly ground black pepper
- ¾ cup oil-packed sun-dried tomatoes, drained (about 4½ ounces)
- ¾ cup olive oil
- 2 tablespoons minced fresh rosemary
- 2 tablespoons minced fresh thyme
- 3 garlic cloves, minced
- 1 teaspoon Tabasco Pepper Sauce

SAUCE

- 1 4-ounce package goat cheese
- 3 garlic cloves, minced
- ½ cup light cream or half-and-half
- ¼ teaspoon Tabasco Garlic Pepper Sauce

- 1 fresh rosemary sprig

For the lamb: Preheat the broiler with the rack 3 to 4 inches from the heat and roast and peel the peppers as described on page 33.

Pat the lamb dry. Sprinkle the meat with salt and pepper to taste. Arrange the roasted pepper pieces and sun-dried tomatoes down the center of the lamb, then roll up the lamb, secure it with twine in several places, and set it in a roasting pan. In a bowl, whisk together the oil, rosemary, thyme, garlic, and Tabasco Sauce. Pour the mixture over the lamb, turning to coat. Cover and refrigerate for 24 hours, turning once or twice.

Preheat the oven to 450°F.

Place the uncovered roast in the oven and immediately reduce the heat to 325°F. Cook the lamb for 20 minutes per pound, about 2 hours, or until a meat thermometer registers 125°F for rare or 140°F for medium. Let the lamb stand for 15 minutes before slicing.

Meanwhile, for the sauce: In a small saucepan, whisk together the goat cheese, garlic, cream, and Tabasco Sauce until the mixture is well blended. Whisk over low heat until heated thoroughly.

Arrange the lamb on a platter, garnish with rosemary, and serve with the sauce.

SERVES 8

FINE-TUNING A PALATE

In the mid-1800s, New Orleans was a prosperous Mediterranean-like city that happened to grow up on the banks of the Mississippi River. It was a hectic metropolis filled with high-spirited Creoles of Spanish, French, and Afro-Caribbean descent, and hard-charging newcomers known as "the Americans." Its restaurants and cuisine were as fine as any on the Continent. And it was here that Edmund McIlhenny became a true gourmet, developing his love of fine food, especially condiments, sauces, and spices.

Mustard-Crusted Leg of Lamb

With a name like McIlhenny you know we like lamb. This well-coated leg is good either hot or at room temperature. If there's any left, it makes superb sandwiches.

2 tablespoons olive oil
½ cup Dijon mustard
2 tablespoons Tabasco Soy Sauce
1 garlic clove, minced
¼ teaspoon ground ginger
1 teaspoon dried thyme
1 tablespoon chopped fresh chives
1 leg of lamb (6 pounds)
½ cup fine dried bread crumbs

In a medium bowl, combine the oil, mustard, Tabasco Soy Sauce, garlic, ginger, thyme, and chives. Place the lamb on a rack in a roasting pan. Coat the lamb with the mustard mixture, sprinkle it with the bread crumbs, and let it stand for 1 hour.

Preheat the oven to 350°F. Roast the lamb for 1 hour 30 minutes, or until a meat thermometer registers 130°F for medium-rare or 145°F for medium.

SERVES 8

> **TIP** **A MUST FOR MEAT**
> A splash of Tabasco Sauce is just the ticket for beef, veal, pork, lamb, and venison dishes. Brush it on the outsides of roasts, steaks, and chops; mix into burgers, meat loaf, meatballs, stews, stir-fries, chili, hash, and casseroles; splash it into marinades and barbecue sauces. Figure on ¼ teaspoon per pound of meat.

UNCLE NED SAVES THE EGRETS

At the turn of the twentieth century, my great-uncle Edward Avery McIlhenny, Grandpère's second son and a naturalist, returned from an Arctic expedition to find that the snowy egrets were almost gone from the Louisiana swamps, victims of the fashion of feathery aigrette plumes on ladies' hats.

After searching for weeks, he found eight young egrets, which he took back to Avery Island and raised in a large cage, releasing them in the fall to migrate across the Gulf of Mexico. Six returned the next spring, forming the nucleus of a bird colony that now numbers in the tens of thousands. Over his life, Uncle Ned banded more than 200,000 birds, crucial in mapping the North American migratory routes.

Uncle Ned succeeded Uncle John as president of the company in 1898. He was a visionary conservationist who persuaded the Rockefeller Foundation and the heiress Mrs. Russell Sage to give Louisiana about 175,000 acres of marshland as wintering grounds for the millions of migratory waterfowl following the Mississippi flyway.

Uncle Ned created the beautiful Jungle Gardens, a 170-acre collection of semitropical trees and plants, on Avery Island, and when oil was discovered in 1942 he insisted that the integrity of the Island's appearance and its role as a wildlife refuge be preserved. Live oak trees were bypassed, pipelines buried or painted green, and in this manner the natural beauty of the island was maintained.

SIDES & SAUCES

Mellow Cabbage Salad

This cabbage slaw, enriched with mustard, herbs, and honey, is excellent served alongside meat, poultry, or fish.

½ teaspoon salt
   Freshly ground black pepper
1 tablespoon cider vinegar
1 tablespoon beef broth (optional)
2 tablespoons Dijon mustard
1 tablespoon honey
1 teaspoon Tabasco *SWEET & Spicy* Sauce
½ teaspoon Tabasco Pepper Sauce
¼ cup olive oil
4 cups finely shredded green cabbage
3 tablespoons chopped green onions
2 tablespoons chopped fresh dill
1 teaspoon celery seed

In a large bowl, whisk together the salt, pepper, vinegar, broth (if using), mustard, honey, and both Tabasco Sauces. Slowly whisk in the oil. Add the remaining ingredients and toss well to blend. Cover and chill. Serve with additional Tabasco Sauce, if desired.

SERVES 4 TO 6

 TIP One-quarter teaspoon of Tabasco Sauce perks up any salad dressing. Use more for a spicier taste.

Sumatra Salad

This simple but rather exotic composed salad marries crisp fresh vegetables and smooth tofu with a spicy peanut dressing for an unusual Indonesian-inspired taste.

SALAD

1 pound green beans

2 cups shredded green cabbage

2 large carrots, cut into thin matchsticks

1 cucumber, cut on the diagonal into ¼-inch slices

1 cup bean sprouts

8 ounces firm tofu, cut into ½-inch cubes

DRESSING

⅓ cup creamy peanut butter

⅓ cup water

2 tablespoons fresh lemon juice

1¼ teaspoons Tabasco Pepper Sauce

½ teaspoon salt

1 garlic clove, halved

1 strip of lemon zest, about 1 inch

¼ cup vanilla yogurt

For the salad: In a vegetable steamer, cook the beans, cabbage, and carrots for 2 to 3 minutes, or until crisp-tender, and cool. Arrange the cooked vegetables, cucumber, sprouts, and tofu on a serving platter.

For the dressing: In a small saucepan, mix together the peanut butter, water, lemon juice, Tabasco Sauce, salt, garlic, and lemon zest, and stir over low heat until smooth. Remove from the heat and discard the garlic and lemon zest. Stir in the yogurt. Serve the dressing warm over the salad.

SERVES 4 TO 6

Spirited Squash

Onion, thyme, and Tabasco Sauce liven up butternut squash in this simple but very good recipe.

1   butternut squash (about 1¾ pounds), peeled and seeded
¼   cup water
¼   cup chopped onion
½   teaspoon dried thyme
1   tablespoon butter
¼   teaspoon salt
½   teaspoon Tabasco Pepper Sauce

Cut the squash into 1-inch cubes. In a medium saucepan, combine the squash, water, onion, and thyme. Cover the pan tightly and cook over low heat for 20 to 25 minutes, or until the squash is tender. Mash the squash with the butter, salt, and Tabasco Sauce.

SERVES 4

Note: To microwave, combine the squash, 2 tablespoons water, the onion, and thyme in a medium microwave-safe dish. Cover and cook on high for 8 to 10 minutes, or until the squash is tender. Mash the squash. Stir in the butter, salt, and Tabasco Sauce.

Honey-Glazed Carrots

Carrots are far from common when teamed with golden raisins, honey, lemon, ginger, and almonds. Tabasco Pepper Sauce effectively balances the sweet flavors.

- 1 **pound carrots, thinly sliced**
- ¼ **cup golden raisins**
- 2 **tablespoons butter**
- 3 **tablespoons honey**
- 1 **tablespoon fresh lemon juice**
- ¼ **teaspoon ground ginger**
- 1 **teaspoon Tabasco** *SWEET & Spicy* **Sauce**
- ¼ **teaspoon Tabasco Pepper Sauce**
- ¼ **cup sliced almonds (optional)**

Preheat the oven to 375°F.

In a medium saucepan, bring ½ inch water to a boil. Add the carrots, cover, and cook over medium heat for 8 minutes, until just tender. Drain the carrots, then transfer to a 1-quart baking dish. Stir in the raisins, butter, honey, lemon juice, ginger, and both Tabasco Sauces. Bake, uncovered, for 25 to 30 minutes, or until the carrots are glazed, stirring occasionally. Spoon into a serving bowl. Sprinkle with almonds, if desired.

SERVES 4

Note: To microwave, combine the butter, honey, lemon juice, ginger, and Tabasco Sauce in a 1½-quart microwave-safe casserole. Microwave on high for 45 seconds, until the butter is melted. Stir to blend. Stir in the carrots. Cover and microwave on high for 8 to 10 minutes, stirring after 4 minutes. Remove from the microwave. Sprinkle with almonds, if desired.

Cheese Scones

Hot from the oven, these scones are really good eating, especially with vegetable soup. To vary the flavor, throw in a half cup chopped reconstituted sun-dried tomatoes, make them with Cheddar cheese instead of Parmesan, or try other herbs such as basil or dill.

2 cups all-purpose flour
¾ cup grated Parmesan cheese
2 teaspoons baking powder
1 teaspoon dried oregano, crumbled
¼ teaspoon salt
4 tablespoons (½ stick) cold butter, cut into pieces
2 large eggs
½ cup whole milk
1 teaspoon Tabasco Pepper Sauce
¾ cup finely chopped onion

Preheat the oven to 400°F. Lightly butter a baking sheet.

In a large bowl or a food processor, mix together the flour, Parmesan, baking powder, oregano, and salt. Cut in the butter, using a pastry blender, or pulses of the food processor, until the mixture resembles coarse crumbs. If blended in a food processor, transfer the mixture to a large bowl.

In a small bowl, lightly beat the eggs. Beat in the milk and Tabasco Sauce. Make a well in the center of the dry ingredients and add the milk mixture, stirring to combine. Mix in the onion. The dough will be sticky.

With lightly floured hands, pat the dough into a 9-inch round in the center of the prepared baking sheet. Cut the round into 8 wedges. Bake the scones for 20 to 25 minutes, or until golden.

MAKES 8

Louisiana Yam Muffins

Coffee, cinnamon, and Tabasco Pepper Sauce give these yam muffins a marvelous and unusual flavor. When you're mashing up yams or sweet potatoes for dinner, remember to save some to make these easy muffins the next day. If you wish, add a half cup chopped pecans to the batter.

1	cup all-purpose flour
1	cup stone-ground yellow cornmeal
¼	cup sugar
1	tablespoon baking powder
1¼	teaspoons ground cinnamon
½	teaspoon salt
2	large eggs
½	cup cold strong coffee
4	tablespoons (½ stick) butter, melted
1	cup mashed cooked yams or sweet potatoes
½	teaspoon Tabasco Pepper Sauce

Preheat the oven to 425°F. Grease twelve 3 x 1½-inch muffin cups.

In a large bowl, mix together the flour, cornmeal, sugar, baking powder, cinnamon, and salt. In a medium bowl, lightly beat the eggs. Stir in the coffee, melted butter, yams, and Tabasco Sauce. Make a well in the center of the dry ingredients. Add the yam mixture and stir just to combine.

TIP

LUNCHTIME LIFTERS
A miniature bottle of Tabasco Sauce (available online) is a cheerful addition to a lunch box, or tuck it into a pocket when traveling. Sprinkle a drop or two of Tabasco Sauce on meat and cheese sandwiches. Add it to chicken, tuna, egg, or potato salad, coleslaw, and deviled eggs. Use a few drops to enliven the mayonnaise or dressing used for sandwiches.

Spoon the batter into the muffin cups and bake for 20 to 25 minutes, or until a cake tester inserted in the center comes out clean. Cool in the pan on a wire rack for 5 minutes, then remove the muffins from the pans. Serve warm or at room temperature.

MAKES 12

Note: To microwave the muffins, spoon about ⅓ cup of batter into each of 6 microwave-safe muffin pan cups or 6-ounce custard cups lined with paper baking cups. Giving the cups or muffin pan half a turn once during cooking, cook, uncovered, on high for 4 to 5½ minutes, until a cake tester inserted in the center comes out clean. Cool for 5 minutes on a wire rack, then remove from the pans. Repeat with the remaining batter.

Pepper mash used in making Tabasco Sauce is aged for three years in white oak barrels.

Okra Creole Style

The tapered green pods called okra, or *févi*, came to Louisiana from Africa. In this dish, okra's rich, earthy flavor is enhanced by traditional Creole vegetables and a splash of Tabasco Sauce. For best results, simmer the okra slowly until tender.

1   tablespoon butter
1   onion, minced
1   garlic clove, minced
1   green bell pepper, finely chopped
3   tomatoes, peeled, seeded, and chopped, juices reserved
1   teaspoon chopped fresh parsley
½   teaspoon Tabasco Pepper Sauce
¾   teaspoon salt
    Freshly ground black pepper
1½ pounds (about 4 dozen) fresh okra, washed and trimmed

In a large nonaluminum saucepan, melt the butter over medium heat. Add the onion, garlic, and bell pepper and cook for 4 to 5 minutes, or until tender. Add the tomatoes and their juices, the parsley, Tabasco Sauce, salt, and pepper to taste. Add the okra, cover, and simmer over low heat for 45 minutes, or until the okra is tender.

SERVES 6

TIP **OKRA**

Okra, a vegetable long prized in Africa, was originally called *guingombo* or *gumbo*, a word that has come to mean the okra-thickened soup and even the soup when it does not contain okra. In Louisiana, fresh, young, tender okra, with its delicious earthy flavor, is served up fried, boiled, and braised, as well as in soups, stews, and innumerable other Cajun and Creole dishes.

Corn Maque Choux

A Cajun classic, maque choux is a good example of a simple vegetable (corn) stepped up in flavor with the addition of traditional Cajun ingredients: onion, green pepper, tomato, and Tabasco Sauce. (See photograph on page 102.)

> 1 tablespoon butter
> ½ cup chopped onion
> ½ cup chopped green bell pepper
> 4 cups whole-kernel corn
>   (canned, fresh, or thawed frozen)
> 1 tomato, seeded and chopped
> ¼ teaspoon salt
> ½ teaspoon Tabasco Pepper Sauce

In a 2-quart saucepan, melt the butter over medium heat. Add the onion and bell pepper and cook, stirring frequently, for 5 minutes, or until tender. Stir in the corn, tomato, salt, and Tabasco Sauce. Reduce the heat and simmer for 10 to 15 minutes, or until the corn is tender.

SERVES 4 TO 6

Spanish Potato Salad

An unusual combination of potatoes, oranges, and red onion tossed with a piquant sauce sets this potato salad apart from the masses.

- 1 **pound new potatoes, scrubbed**
- 3 **cups salad greens, torn into small pieces**
- ¼ **cup sliced celery**
- 1 **medium red onion, thinly sliced**
- 2 **navel oranges, peeled and sectioned**
- ¼ **cup mayonnaise**
- ¼ **cup plain yogurt**
- 2 **tablespoons orange juice**
- ½ **teaspoon Tabasco Pepper Sauce**
- ½ **teaspoon salt**

Fill a medium saucepan with 1½ inches of salted water and bring to a boil. Add the potatoes, cover, and cook for 30 minutes, or until fork-tender. Drain, cool, and cut into ¼-inch slices.

Line a salad bowl with the greens. On the greens, layer the potatoes, celery, onion, and orange sections. Chill.

In a small bowl, beat together the mayonnaise, yogurt, orange juice, Tabasco Sauce, and salt. Just before serving, toss the salad with the dressing.

SERVES 4

TIP Pile your favorite toppings on a baked potato, like cheese, broccoli, and sour cream, then top it all off with a few drops of Tabasco Sauce.

Red Beans and Rice on Monday

In New Orleans, red beans and rice has evolved into a traditional Monday dish, but it's a fine accompaniment any time for fried chicken, pork chops, ham, or sausage.

- 1 pound dried red beans, rinsed and picked over
- 8 cups cold water
- ½ pound lean salt pork, bacon, or ham, diced
- 1 tablespoon olive oil
- 1 cup chopped onion
- 1 garlic clove, minced
- 2 tablespoons chopped fresh parsley
- ¾ teaspoon salt
- 1½ teaspoons Tabasco Pepper Sauce
- 4 cups hot cooked rice, for serving

Soak the beans overnight in a large saucepan with enough water to cover. Drain and add the beans with the 8 cups water to the saucepan. Add the pork, bacon, or ham and bring to a simmer. Cook, covered, for 15 minutes.

Meanwhile, in a medium skillet, heat the oil over medium heat. Add the onion and garlic and cook for 3 minutes, or until golden.

Add the onion mixture to the beans along with the parsley, salt, and Tabasco Sauce. Cover and simmer for 1 hour 30 minutes to 1 hour 45 minutes, or until the beans are tender enough to mash easily with a fork. Add hot water as needed to keep the beans covered, and stir occasionally. When the beans are finished they will have soaked up most of the liquid.

Serve over the hot cooked rice.

SERVES 8

Lemon-Sesame Asparagus

This simple butter sauce brings out the best in fresh asparagus. The sesame seeds add crunch and the Tabasco Sauce and lemon contribute a little bite.

2 pounds asparagus, trimmed
1 tablespoon butter
2 teaspoons sesame seeds
2 tablespoons fresh lemon juice
¼ teaspoon salt
¼ teaspoon Tabasco Pepper Sauce
Lemon wedges, for garnish

In a vegetable steamer, cook the asparagus for 5 to 10 minutes, just until crisp-tender. Transfer to a heated serving dish and keep warm.

Meanwhile, in a small skillet, combine the butter and sesame seeds over medium heat for 3 to 4 minutes, or until the sesame seeds are browned. Stir in the lemon juice, salt, and Tabasco Sauce.

Pour the sauce over the asparagus and garnish with lemon wedges.

SERVES 4

Herb-Broiled Tomatoes

Quick and colorful, these are an attractive accompaniment to meat, chicken, or fish.

> 4 tomatoes
> ½ teaspoon salt
> ½ teaspoon sugar
> ½ teaspoon Tabasco Pepper Sauce
> 1 tablespoon butter, melted
> ¼ cup fine dried bread crumbs
> ¼ teaspoon dried basil
> ¼ teaspoon dried thyme
> Chopped fresh parsley, for garnish

Position a rack 4 inches from the heat and preheat the broiler.

Cut the tops off the tomatoes. Place them cut side up on a broiler pan and sprinkle with the salt and sugar.

In a small bowl, blend the Tabasco Sauce with the butter, then add the bread crumbs, basil, and thyme. Spoon the mixture over the tomatoes. Broil for about 5 minutes until bread crumbs are golden and tomatoes are fork-tender. Serve sprinkled with parsley.

SERVES 4

Zydeco Green Beans

The name Zydeco Green Beans is actually a redundancy. The exuberant music of Louisiana's black French-speaking Creoles is called "zydeco," an idiomatic phonetic version of *les haricots*, French for snap beans. Serve these green beans as a relish, or as "stirrers" for a Bloody Mary (page 50).

2¼	cups water
¾	cup distilled white vinegar
2	tablespoons sugar
1	tablespoon mustard seeds, crushed
4	garlic cloves, thinly sliced
3	bay leaves
1½	teaspoons salt
1½	teaspoons Tabasco Pepper Sauce
1	pound green beans

In a large saucepan, stir together the water, vinegar, sugar, mustard seeds, garlic, bay leaves, salt, and Tabasco Sauce. Bring to a boil, reduce the heat, cover, and simmer for 5 minutes. Add the beans. Cover and simmer for 10 minutes, until crisp-tender.

Arrange the beans in a shallow dish and cover them completely with the vinegar mixture. Cover and refrigerate overnight. Serve cold.

MAKES 1 QUART

Trapper's Camp Beans

Even Louisiana has its cold days, when we look forward to a dish that warms the insides. This cassoulet-like dish is an authoritative one-pot meal that includes leeks and carrots along with sausage. Adding more Tabasco Sauce at the table really gives it zing.

1 pound dried beans (Great Northern, yellow eye, or pinto), rinsed and picked over

4½ cups cold water

¼ pound unsliced bacon or salt pork

2 leeks (white part only), thinly sliced and well washed

2 cups chopped onion

1 whole onion, peeled

6 whole cloves

1 14.5-ounce can chicken broth

5 carrots, cut into 1-inch pieces

3 garlic cloves, minced

2 teaspoons Tabasco Pepper Sauce

1 teaspoon dried marjoram

1 teaspoon dried sage

1 teaspoon dried thyme

2 bay leaves

6 black peppercorns

1 14.5-ounce can whole tomatoes, crushed

1 pound Polish sausage, cut into ½-inch slices

In a 6-quart Dutch oven or heavy ovenproof pot, soak the beans in the water overnight. Do not drain the beans.

In a skillet, brown the bacon or salt pork on both sides over medium heat. Remove the meat and drain on paper towels.

Add the leeks and chopped onion to the skillet and cook for 10 minutes, or until tender. Add the bacon or salt pork, leeks, and chopped onion to the beans. Stud the whole onion with the cloves and add to the beans. Add the broth, carrots, garlic, Tabasco Sauce, marjoram, sage, thyme, bay leaves, and peppercorns to the beans. Bring to a boil, reduce the heat, cover, and simmer for 1 hour, stirring occasionally.

Preheat the oven to 350°F.

Stir in the tomatoes and sausage and bake the casserole, uncovered, for 1 hour, or until almost all the liquid is absorbed.

SERVES 6 TO 8

BEANS

Beans—red, white, string, or lima—have always been a mainstay in Louisiana, and become particularly flavorful with the addition of pepper sauce. Red beans and rice is a typical Monday dish, the beans simmered with the Sunday hambone, served over rice, and topped with a sprinkling of green onions. Red beans are also cooked with red wine and sausage, pork, or ham, or puréed with butter, milk, and cream to the consistency of mashed potatoes. White beans, cooked in a similar fashion, are popular with Creoles for their more delicate flavor and texture. Add a generous dash of Tabasco Sauce to any bean dish, and offer additional Tabasco Sauce at the table.

Pickled Shallots

We keep a container of these in the refrigerator to serve as a relish with cold cuts, steak, hamburgers, chicken, and a variety of other meat dishes.

- 3 pounds small shallots or pearl onions
- 2 cups distilled white vinegar
- 2 cups water
- 6 tablespoons sugar
- 2 teaspoons crumbled dried rosemary
- 2 teaspoons salt
- 1 teaspoon Tabasco Pepper Sauce

Drop the shallots (or pearl onions) into a large pot of boiling water and cook for 1 minute. Drain and rinse with cold water. Cut off the roots, slip off the skins, and set aside.

In a large saucepan, combine the vinegar, water, sugar,

rosemary, salt, and Tabasco Sauce and simmer for 3 minutes. Add the shallots and simmer for 15 minutes, until crisp-tender. Cool them slightly, then cover and refrigerate for 2 to 3 days to blend the flavors. They may be kept refrigerated in sealed containers for several weeks. Serve the shallots at room temperature.

MAKES 6 CUPS

Hot Pepper Jelly

We generally make our pepper jelly—a favorite at the Country Store—with aged Tabasco pepper mash from the factory to give it color and flavor. Although perhaps not quite as fiery, this simple recipe using the pepper sauce makes a mellow, spicy jelly. Spread cream cheese on crackers, then top with a dollop of the jelly for a tempting morsel to serve with cocktails. Pectin is available in well-stocked supermarkets.

4	large red or green bell peppers, cut into large pieces
1½	teaspoons Tabasco Pepper Sauce
¾	cup cider vinegar
3½	cups sugar
1	3-ounce pouch liquid fruit pectin

In a food processor or blender, coarsely chop the peppers. In a large nonaluminum saucepan, combine the peppers, Tabasco Sauce, vinegar, and sugar. Bring to a boil over high heat and boil rapidly for 10 minutes, stirring occasionally. Remove from the heat and stir in the pectin. Return the pan to the heat and return to a boil. Boil the jelly for exactly 1 minute, stirring frequently (to prevent bits of pepper from rising to the surface) and skimming the foam off the top. Then remove from the heat.

Ladle the jelly into hot sterilized ½-pint jelly jars, seal, and place on a rack in a deep kettle. Pour boiling water over the jars to cover by 2 inches and bring to a boil over high heat. Continue to boil for 10 minutes, then transfer to a rack to cool.

MAKES 6 HALF-PINTS

Dirty Rice

An original soul food, dirty rice is cooked white rice mixed up with chopped chicken giblets and well-seasoned vegetables. It makes a great poultry stuffing.

½   pound chicken gizzards
½   pound chicken livers
2   tablespoons olive oil
½   cup chopped onion
⅓   cup chopped celery
⅓   cup chopped green bell pepper
2   garlic cloves, minced
1½ teaspoons salt
½   teaspoon freshly ground black pepper
1½ teaspoons Tabasco Pepper Sauce
2   cups water
1   tablespoon butter
1   cup raw long-grain white rice
½   cup chopped green onions

To chop the gizzards and livers, freeze them for at least 30 minutes so they are easier to handle, then finely chop them, keeping them separate.

In a large skillet, heat the oil over medium heat. Add the gizzards and cook for 5 minutes. Add the onion, celery, green pepper, garlic, ½ teaspoon of the salt, and the pepper, and cook for 10 minutes until vegetables are tender, stirring occasionally. Add the livers and Tabasco Sauce and cook over low heat for 20 minutes longer, stirring occasionally, until meat is tender.

Meanwhile, in a medium saucepan, combine the water, butter, and remaining 1 teaspoon salt. Bring the mixture to a boil and stir in the rice. Cover, then reduce the heat and simmer for 20 minutes, or until the liquid is absorbed and the rice is tender.

Combine the rice and giblet mixture, and stir in the chopped green onions. Serve hot.

SERVES 6 TO 8

HOT PEPPERS **COMBAT THE COMMON COLD**

People visiting the Tabasco Sauce factory on Avery Island can expect to get their heads cleared when they take a whiff of the sauce being stirred. In fact, eating fiery foods can actually relieve congestion in the nose, sinuses, and lungs. Dr. Irwin Ziment, professor emeritus of clinical medicine at the University of California at Los Angeles, recommends a glass of tomato juice laced with ten to twenty drops of Tabasco Pepper Sauce, taken several times daily, as an excellent decongestant.

Barrels of aging pepper mash in an Avery Island warehouse.

Peppery Polenta with Tangy Tomato Sauce

This is our version of Italian polenta, punched up with Tabasco Sauce and served with a fresh tomato herb sauce. It's fabulous as a main dish or served on the side with meat or chicken.

POLENTA

4 tablespoons butter

½ cup chopped onion

4¼ cups water

1⅓ cups cornmeal

½ teaspoon salt

¾ teaspoon Tabasco Pepper Sauce

TANGY TOMATO SAUCE

¼ cup extra-virgin olive oil

1 cup coarsely chopped onion

2 cloves garlic, minced

3 pounds tomatoes, peeled, seeded, and chopped

2 tablespoons chopped fresh basil leaves or 1 tablespoon dried basil

1 teaspoon dried oregano

1 teaspoon Tabasco Pepper Sauce

½ teaspoon salt

Freshly grated Parmesan cheese (optional)

Preheat the oven to 375°F.

For the polenta: In a medium saucepan, melt 2 tablespoons of the butter over medium heat. Add the onion and cook for 5 minutes, or until golden. Stir in the water and bring to a boil. Gradually add the cornmeal, stirring constantly. Add the salt and Tabasco Sauce. Stir the polenta over low heat for 15 minutes, or until the mixture is very thick.

> **TIP**
>
> ## GREAT GRAINS
>
> Grains are nutritious and comforting, but lack mouth-filling flavor on their own. Just ¼ teaspoon of Tabasco Sauce per cup added to the cooking liquid really heightens their taste. Try it with bulgur, polenta, wild rice, and white or brown dishes such as risotto and pilaf.

On the stovetop or in the microwave, melt the remaining 2 tablespoons butter. Brush a 1½-quart shallow round baking dish with half of it. Turn the polenta into the dish and brush the remaining melted butter on top. Bake for 30 to 40 minutes, or until lightly browned.

Meanwhile, for the tangy tomato sauce: In a large heavy skillet, heat the oil on medium. Add the onion and garlic and cook for 5 minutes, or until tender. Add the tomatoes, basil, oregano, Tabasco Sauce, and salt. Bring to a boil, reduce the heat, and simmer for 20 minutes to blend flavors.

To serve, cut the polenta into wedges and sprinkle with Parmesan cheese, if desired. Serve with the sauce.

SERVES 6 TO 8

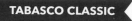

Paul McIlhenny's Lemon and Garlic Grilling Sauce

This is my favorite sauce for basting beef, chicken, or pork cooked on the grill or under the broiler. I often put the squeezed half lemon into the pot to simmer with the juice for extra flavor. In this and all recipes calling for Worcestershire sauce, I prefer Lea & Perrins or even our own Tabasco brand, but you can make your own selection.

  8 **tablespoons (1 stick) butter**
 ½ **lemon**
  1 **tablespoon Tabasco Worcestershire Sauce**
  1 **teaspoon Tabasco Pepper Sauce**
  3 **garlic cloves, minced**
 ¼ **teaspoon salt**
     Freshly ground black pepper

In a nonaluminum medium saucepan, melt the butter over low heat. Squeeze the lemon juice into the pan and bring the mixture to a slow simmer. Add the Tabasco Worcestershire Sauce and Tabasco Sauce. Stir in the garlic and continue to simmer for 10 minutes. Add the salt and pepper to taste.

MAKES ¾ CUP

Hot Damn Pesto

A variation on pesto, this recipe combines parsley, watercress, and basil in a sprightly sauce that can be drizzled on cold cooked shrimp, salmon, carpaccio, or warmed and tossed with hot pasta.

1	cup packed fresh parsley, rinsed and dried
1	cup packed watercress leaves, rinsed and dried
1	cup packed fresh basil leaves, rinsed and dried
¼	cup pine nuts or almonds, toasted
¼	cup fresh lime juice
¼	cup olive oil
2	small garlic cloves
1	tablespoon Tabasco Green Jalapeño Sauce
1	teaspoon Tabasco Pepper Sauce

In a food processor or blender, combine all of the ingredients and process until smooth. Transfer the sauce to a covered container and chill for at least 24 hours to develop the flavors.

SERVES 4

Avery Island Barbecue Sauce

This classic spicy barbecue sauce has a mellow, rich flavor that is marvelous with just about anything you'd care to grill. Brush the sauce on chicken, ribs, hotdogs, or hamburgers during grilling—or even when broiling or baking. Serve additional sauce on the side.

- 2 tablespoons butter
- 1 cup chopped onion
- ½ cup chopped celery, with leaves
- ¼ cup chopped green bell pepper
- 1 tablespoon minced garlic
- 2 14.5-ounce cans diced tomatoes, drained
- 1 6-ounce can tomato paste
- ⅓ cup red wine vinegar
- 3 tablespoons molasses
- 2 lemon slices
- 2 teaspoons Tabasco Pepper Sauce
- 2 teaspoons Tabasco Chipotle Sauce
- 2 teaspoons dry mustard
- 1 bay leaf
- ½ teaspoon ground cloves
- ½ teaspoon ground allspice

In a large, heavy nonaluminum saucepan, melt the butter over medium heat. Add the onion, celery, bell pepper, and garlic and cook for 5 minutes, or until the onion is tender but not browned. Add the remaining ingredients. Cover and simmer for 30 minutes, or until the sauce thickens, stirring occasionally. Discard the lemon slices and bay leaf.

MAKES 2¼ CUPS

Rémoulade Sauce

Rémoulade sauce is another Louisiana specialty that varies with the cook. A piquant mustard-based sauce, it is excellent on cold shrimp or crabmeat, and also goes nicely with hot crisp-fried fish or shellfish. Try it spooned over hard-boiled egg halves as an appetizer, or use it as a dip for cooked artichokes.

- ¼ cup spicy coarse-ground mustard
- 2 teaspoons paprika
- 1 teaspoon Tabasco Pepper Sauce
- 1 teaspoon salt
- ½ teaspoon freshly ground black pepper
- ¼ cup tarragon vinegar
- 1 cup olive oil
- ½ cup coarsely chopped green onions
- ½ cup finely chopped celery
- ¼ cup finely chopped fresh parsley

In a medium bowl, whisk together the mustard, paprika, Tabasco Sauce, salt, and pepper. Beat in the vinegar. Then, whisking constantly, add the oil in a slow, thin stream, continuing to beat until the sauce is thick and smooth. Stir in the green onions, celery, and parsley and mix well. Cover and refrigerate the bowl, letting the sauce stand for at least 2 hours before serving to allow the flavors to blend.

MAKES 2 CUPS

> **TIP** Adding ¼ teaspoon of Tabasco Sauce gives a pleasing tang to Hollandaise, Béarnaise, or white sauce.

DESSERTS

Smoldering Swirled Brownies

Sweet loves spice, and in this chocolate cream cheese brownie recipe the two combine in perfect harmony.

CREAM CHEESE MIXTURE

- 3 ounces cream cheese, at room temperature
- 2 tablespoons butter, at room temperature
- ¼ cup sugar
- 1 large egg
- 3 tablespoons all-purpose flour
- 1 teaspoon Tabasco Pepper Sauce

CHOCOLATE MIXTURE

- 8 tablespoons (1 stick) butter
- 2 ounces (2 squares) unsweetened chocolate
- 2 large eggs
- ¾ cup sugar
- ⅓ cup all-purpose flour
- 2 teaspoons Tabasco Pepper Sauce
- 2 teaspoons vanilla extract
- ½ teaspoon salt

Preheat the oven to 350°F. Grease an 8-inch square baking pan.

For the cream cheese mixture: In a bowl, with an electric mixer, beat the cream cheese and butter at medium speed until smooth. Add the sugar, egg, flour, and Tabasco Sauce and beat until well mixed. Set aside.

For the chocolate mixture: In a medium microwave-safe bowl, melt the butter and chocolate. Set aside to cool slightly. Then beat in the eggs, sugar, flour, Tabasco Sauce, vanilla, and salt. Stir until just blended.

Spoon the chocolate mixture into the prepared pan. Spoon

the cream cheese mixture in dollops on top of the chocolate mixture. Cut and twist through the two mixtures a few times with a small spatula to create a swirl effect.

Bake the brownies for 35 to 40 minutes, or until set. Cool completely in the pan, then cut into 16 squares.

MAKES 16 BROWNIES

Blistering Brittle

A Southern favorite, brittles are made to be very sweet. This version uses Tabasco Sauce to cut the cloying sweetness and bring out the peanut flavor.

Cooking spray
1 tablespoon butter, melted
1 tablespoon Tabasco Green Jalapeño Sauce
½ teaspoon ground allspice
1½ cups dry-roasted peanuts
1 cup sugar
½ cup light corn syrup
½ cup water

Lightly coat a spatula and large baking sheet with cooking spray. Set aside.

In a large bowl, combine the butter, Tabasco Sauce, and allspice and mix well. Add the peanuts and toss well.

In a 2-quart microwave-safe bowl, combine the sugar, corn syrup, and water and stir with a wooden spoon until well mixed. Microwave, uncovered, on high for 3 minutes. Remove from the microwave and stir thoroughly.

Stir in the peanut mixture. Cover the bowl tightly with microwavable plastic wrap and microwave on high for 12 to 15 minutes, or until the peanuts and syrup are amber colored. Remove the bowl from the microwave. Pierce the plastic with the tip of sharp knife (to release steam) and uncover carefully. Pour the mixture onto the prepared baking sheet and let harden. When cool, break into pieces.

MAKES ABOUT 1½ POUNDS

Peppery Gingerbread

This holiday favorite is known for its pungent taste and smell, which is intensified here with the addition of Tabasco Sauce. The recipe below provides a fluffier cakelike gingerbread, not the flat rigid kind used for tabletop architectural masterpieces.

2   cups all-purpose flour, plus more for the pan
1   cup light molasses
¾   cup whole milk
½   cup granulated sugar
½   cup butter, at room temperature
1   tablespoon Tabasco Pepper Sauce
1½ teaspoons ground ginger
1   teaspoon ground cinnamon
1   teaspoon baking soda
1   large egg
    Confectioners' sugar, for sprinkling

Preheat the oven to 325°F. Grease and flour a 9-inch square baking pan.

In a large bowl, with an electric mixer, beat together the flour, molasses, milk, granulated sugar, butter, Tabasco Sauce, ginger, cinnamon, baking soda, and egg at low speed until well blended and smooth. Increase the speed to medium and beat for 2 minutes, occasionally scraping the bowl with a rubber spatula.

Pour the batter into the prepared pan. Bake for 1 hour, or until a cake tester inserted in the center comes out clean. Cool in the pan on a wire rack.

Sprinkle the top of the gingerbread with confectioners' sugar.

SERVES 12

Spicy Pumpkin Tart

In this recipe, Tabasco intensifies the flavors of traditional pumpkin pie, highlighting the earthy pumpkin, bright ginger, and deep cinnamon and nutmeg. A pecan crust celebrates what is in season in the fall.

CRUST

1¼ cups all-purpose flour
½ cup ground pecans
⅓ cup granulated sugar
¼ teaspoon ground cinnamon
½ cup butter, at room temperature

FILLING

1 15-ounce can unsweetened pumpkin purée
2 large eggs
¾ cup packed light brown sugar
¾ cup half-and-half
1 teaspoon ground cinnamon
1 teaspoon Tabasco Pepper Sauce
½ teaspoon ground ginger
½ teaspoon ground nutmeg

Whole pecans, for garnish (optional)
Whipped cream, for serving (optional)

For the crust: Preheat the oven to 400°F.

In a large bowl, combine the flour, ground pecans, granulated sugar, and cinnamon. Stir in the softened butter until well blended. Press the mixture into bottom and up the sides of a 9-inch fluted tart pan with a removable bottom. Prick the crust with a fork in a few places. Bake for 10 minutes, or until the crust is slightly set.

Meanwhile, for the filling: In a large bowl, combine the pumpkin, eggs, brown sugar, half-and-half, cinnamon, Tabasco Sauce, ginger, and nutmeg and mix well.

Spoon the filling into the partially baked crust. Reduce the oven temperature to 350°F and bake for 30 minutes, or until the filling is set. Transfer to a wire rack to cool.

To serve, garnish tart with pecans and whipped cream, if desired.

SERVES 8

Hot Bananas with Rum and Chocolate

This take on Bananas Foster swaps in Tabasco Sauce for the usual cinnamon.

- 2 tablespoons butter
- 2 tablespoons dark brown sugar
- 2 tablespoons honey
- ¾ teaspoon Tabasco Pepper Sauce
- ½ teaspoon Tabasco *SWEET & Spicy* Sauce
- 4 ripe bananas, peeled and sliced crosswise into 1-inch rounds
- 3 tablespoons dark rum
- 1 cup vanilla ice cream
- Chocolate-flavored syrup, for drizzling

In a large skillet, combine the butter, brown sugar, honey, and both Tabasco Sauces and cook over medium-high heat until the mixture sizzles. Add the bananas and toss gently until well coated. Increase the heat to high, add the rum, and cook for 20 seconds, or until the mixture has a syrupy consistency and the bananas are glazed.

Scoop ice cream into bowls and spoon the warm bananas on top. Drizzle with chocolate syrup and serve immediately.

SERVES 4

TIP

TABASCO SAUCE IN DESSERTS?
Give desserts a new dash with Tabasco Sauce. Add a teaspoon to your recipe for peanut butter, ginger, or sugar cookies. Sauté bananas in a combination of butter, brown sugar, honey, and a couple of drops of Tabasco Sauce. Add a splash to chocolate or caramel sauce and pour over ice cream or cold cut-up fruit for real taste excitement.

Come Visit Us!

We welcome about 100,000 visitors to Avery Island each year to see Jungle Gardens and its famous Bird City, the Tabasco Visitors Center, and the Tabasco Country Store. We greet each visitor personally and, after the tour, say good-bye with a *lagniappe* (small gift) of a miniature bottle of pepper sauce and a handful of recipes. The Island is about 140 miles west of New Orleans, making it a pleasant day's trip through the bayou country.

MAIL-ORDER SUPPLIERS

Tabasco® brand and McIlhenny Farms® brand products, assorted cookbooks, giftware, and Cajun specialties:

TABASCO® Country Store
1 (800) 634-9599
www.TABASCO.com

Crawfish, oysters, shrimp, crabs, frog legs, alligator, sausages, other meats, seasonings, and other Cajun products:

CajunGrocer
1 (888) 272-9347
www.CajunGrocer.com

Savoie's Real Cajun
1 (337) 942-7241
www.savoiesfoods.com

Louisiana Crawfish Co.
1 (800) 221-8060
www.lacrawfish.com

Broken Arrow Ranch
1 (800) 962-4263
www.brokenarrowranch.com

K-Paul's Louisiana Kitchen
1 (800) 457-2857
www.chefpaul.com

Index

♪♪♪♪

Note: Page references in *italics* indicate photographs.

Breakfast & brunch
  Cheese Grits, 23
  Chicken Hash, 26–27
  Fresh Corn Pudding, 19
  Grillades, 28–29
  Rudy's Cheese Omelets à la Suds, 18
  Shirred Eggs with Sherried
    Mushrooms, 24, *25*
  Spicy Spinach Quichettes, 20, *21*
  Spicy Steak and Eggs Benedict, 22

Desserts
  Blistering Brittle, 136
  Hot Bananas with Rum and Chocolate,
    140
  Peppery Gingerbread, 137
  Smoldering Swirled Brownies, 134–35,
    135
  Spicy Pumpkin Tart, 138–39, *139*
Drinks
  Classic Bloody Mary, 50, *51*
  Melon Cooler, 55
  The Morning After, 52
  Red Snapper, 49
  Sangrita, 53
  Seeing Red Margaritas, 54

Eggs & cheese
  Baked Mac and Cheese, 60–61
  Cheese Grits, 23
  Cheese Scones, *108,* 109
  Rudy's Cheese Omelets à la Suds, 18
  Shirred Eggs with Sherried
    Mushrooms, 24, *25*
  Spicy Spinach and Artichoke Dip, 34
  Spicy Spinach Quichettes, 20, *21*
  Spicy Steak and Eggs Benedict, 22

Grains & beans
  Cheese Grits, 23
  Cornmeal Nips, 40
  Dirty Rice, 124–25
  Eula Mae's Jambalaya, 80–81
  Peppery Polenta with Tangy Tomato
    Sauce, 126–27
  Red Beans and Rice on Monday, 115
  Sumatra Salad, 105
  Trapper's Camp Beans, 120–21
  Zydeco Green Beans, 119

McIlhenny, Edmund, 12–13, *13,* 99
McIlhenny, Edward, 101, *101*
McIlhenny, John, 45, 101
McIlhenny, Paul, 8–9, 10–11
McIlhenny, Walter, 61, *61,* 93
Meat & poultry
  Chicken and Andouille Gumbo,
    64–65
  Chicken Hash, 26–27
  Chicken Olé Mole, 82–83
  Eula Mae's Jambalaya, 80–81
  Fried Chicken, 84, *85*
  Gingered Pork Roast, 94–95
  Grillades, 28–29
  Hot 'n' Spicy Chicken Wings with Blue
    Cheese Dip, 44–45
  Individual Sugar Snap Pea and
    Chicken Pot Pies, 86–87
  Jalapeño Pork Tacos with Pineapple
    Salsa and Pickled Onion, *96,* 97
  Mustard-Crusted Leg of Lamb, 100
  Pepper-Stuffed Lamb with Garlic
    Chèvre Sauce, 98–99
  Peppery Sausage and Onion Grilled
    Pizza, 88
  Perfect Seared Steaks, 91
  Spicy Steak and Eggs Benedict, 22
  Sweet and Smoky Baby Back Ribs,
    92–93
  The Ultimate Hamburger, 89
  Walter's Chili, 90

Pasta
  Autumn Harvest Fettuccine, 58, *59*
  Baked Mac and Cheese, 60–61

Sauces
  Barbecue, Avery Island, 130
  Chunky Salsa, 36
  Hot Damn Pesto, 129
  Lemon and Garlic Grilling, Paul
    McIlhenny's, 128
  Rémoulade, 131
Seafood
  Baked Cherrystone Clams with Spicy
    Butter, 41
  Dressed Seafood Po'boys, 72-73
  Eula Mae's Cajun Seafood Gumbo,
    62-63
  Eula Mae's Jambalaya, 80-81
  Fiery Catfish Fingers, 38, 39
  Fred's Hottest Shrimp, 66-67
  Frog Legs Piquant, 76-77
  Hot Grilled Trout, 78
  Judy McIlhenny's Crawfish Étouffée,
    74-75
  MTK's Sauced Shrimp, 37
  Oyster Bisque, 47
  Salmon Steaks with Cucumber Sauce,
    79
  Scallops in Double Pepper Sauce,
    70, 71
  Shrimp Creole, 68-69
  Vermilion Bay Fish Chowder, 48
Sides
  Cheese Scones, 108, 109
  Corn Maque Choux, 102, 113
  Dirty Rice, 124-25
  Herb-Broiled Tomatoes, 118
  Honey-Glazed Carrots, 107
  Hot Pepper Jelly, 123
  Lemon-Sesame Asparagus, 116, 117
  Louisiana Yam Muffins, 110-11
  Mellow Cabbage Salad, 104
  Okra Creole Style, 112
  Peppery Polenta with Tangy Tomato
    Sauce, 126-27

  Pickled Shallots, 122, 122
  Red Beans and Rice on Monday, 115
  Spanish Potato Salad, 114
  Spirited Squash, 106
  Sumatra Salad, 105
  Trapper's Camp Beans, 120-21
  Zydeco Green Beans, 119
Soups & stews
  Chicken and Andouille Gumbo,
    64-65
  Eula Mae's Cajun Seafood Gumbo,
    62-63
  Oyster Bisque, 47
  Potato, Artichoke, and Leek Soup, 46
  Vermilion Bay Fish Chowder, 48
  Walter's Chili, 90
Starters
  Baked Cherrystone Clams with Spicy
    Butter, 41
  Chunky Salsa, 36
  Cornmeal Nips, 40
  Fiery Catfish Fingers, 38, 39
  Guacamole, 35
  Hot 'n' Spicy Chicken Wings with Blue
    Cheese Dip, 44-45
  MTK's Sauced Shrimp, 37
  Peppered Pecans, 32
  Portobello Nachos, 42, 43
  Roasted Red Pepper Dip, 33
  Spicy Spinach and Artichoke Dip, 34

Tabasco Sauce
  capsicum peppers in, 67
  corporate offices, 87
  in England, 55
  global sales of, 73
  in the military, 93
  production of, 12-14
  promotion efforts, 45
  and U.S. presidents, 27

PAUL McILHENNY was the fourth generation of McIlhennys to produce Tabasco Pepper Sauce and the CEO and Chairman of the Board of McIlhenny Company. He was inducted into the James Beard Foundation's Who's Who of Food & Beverage in 2010 as a result of his leadership in the company and in the communities of New Orleans and Avery Island. McIlhenny grew up in New Orleans and lived and cooked on Avery Island for fifty years.

BARBARA HUNTER is the founder of Hunter Public Relations, a New York City–based communications agency specializing in marketing food and beverage brands. Hunter has advised the McIlhenny Company for 45 years.